Memoirs

Memoirs of an Egotist

Stendhal

Translated by Andrew Brown

ET REMOTISSIMA PROPE

100 PAGES

100 PAGES
Published by Hesperus Press Limited
4 Rickett Street, London SW6 1RU
www.hesperuspress.com

Memoirs of an Egotist first published in French as *Souvenirs d'Egotisme* in 1892;
'The Privileges' first published in French as '*Fragment inédit de Stendhal*' in 1861
This translation first published by Hesperus Press Limited, 2003

Introduction and English language translation © Andrew Brown, 2003
Foreword © Doris Lessing, 2003

Designed and typeset by Fraser Muggeridge
Printed in the United Arab Emirates by Oriental Press

ISBN: 1-84391-040-3

CONTENTS

Opening a Stendhal after – you have to think – a far too long interval, there is, at least for me, a rush of exhilaration, as if you have turned a corner and look! – there's an old friend you haven't seen for a time and you have forgotten what an extraordinary being he is. Stendhal said he didn't expect readers who would understand him until 1890; but this was a movable rendezvous with the future. At any rate they were still children or even unborn. This select few are now spread everywhere, but the nature of our fond addiction is perhaps not so simple, nor even entirely blame-free. A clue is in his remark that when he wrote this memoir he was not thirty-eight but more like twenty. And it is true that we may easily recognise our adolescent selves in his prickly self-regard. I was in my twenties when I found *The Red and the Black* – and a friend.

The ideal lover of Stendhal comes, as he did, from a family of conventional people in a provincial town – in his case Grenoble – which is snug, complacent and reactionary, both politically and socially. His family took their social obduracy to an extreme. His beloved mother died when he was seven, and he was brought up by three people he hated. One was a maiden aunt who tormented him; one a despotic Jesuit, who tutored him, and taught him to loathe the church and all its works; and then there was his father, a lawyer, who 'had all the prejudices of religion and aristocracy, [and] vehemently prevented me from studying music.' Without the interventions of his mother's father, a kindly and intelligent man, there would have been no softer influences on his young life. He was not allowed to play with children considered his social inferiors, was treated more like a recalcitrant animal than a child, was harried by injunctions and prohibitions he could never see the sense of. I do not think it irrelevant that at the end of *The Red and the Black*, when Julien Sorel is about to be put to death, the father visits him and complains that Julien has not repaid him the money spent on him for his food and his keep as a child. Monstrous parents and figures of authority abound in his work. Never can there have been anyone more thankful that he has finally grown up and is able to leave home.

He did not keep the snobbishness they tried to teach him, but he remained as sensitive to a different crudeness: the coarseness he hated was not social, but the bruising blunderings of the unkind heart.

'I had an almost rabid fear of any coarse person. The conversation of some coarse fat provincial merchant would stupefy me and make me unhappy for the rest of the entire day.'

Oh yes, the provinces – or, in my case, small-town colonial society – '… the most tedious despotism. It is what is behind this nasty word that makes residence in small towns impossible for those who have lived in that great republic, Paris' (*The Red and the Black*).

This memoir is of a stay in Paris from 1821 to 1830. He wrote imagining it would be read by someone dear to him, 'a person such as Mme Roland or M. Gros, the geometrician'. Here, in a few words, are his passion for mathematics and his need for a sympathetic woman, but in this case she was dead, by the guillotine, whose shadow had to lie across his life and mind and those of his contemporaries, for good or ill: it is hard to sympathise with his enthusiasm for some of its operations. Inevitable, I suppose, that, brought up by tyrants, he applauded the instrument that had brought some tyrants low. The man was a mass of contradictions – and he knew it.

He writes to find out what kind of a being he is. 'What kind of man am I? Do I have common sense, do I have common sense and profundity too? Am I remarkably witty? Truth to tell, I haven't the slightest idea.'

The lens of his intelligence is focused on himself with a concentration that amounts to ferocity. He lists his absurd characteristics as well as his good ones, and never spares himself the description of a moment of humiliation or silliness. He had Rousseau as an admired model, but I think that self-confessor did not come near Stendhal for honest clear-sightedness, which quality is a compensatory gift to a child who has spent years observing, with satirical and unforgiving eyes, the hypocrisies and injustices of grown-ups; who has had, in order to survive, to learn watchfulness, which is the first qualification for a writer. The close observation of their enemies, mother, father, authority figures, teaches these unhappy children how to dissemble or keep silent – and see everything.

Stendhal left Milan, left his beloved Italy, because the Milanese police thought he was a spy. He left behind a love affair – no, a grand passion – that had made him very unhappy, and was unconsummated – though there are hints this might have been his fault. But if he had been happy we would not have had his book *On Love*, which he was to finish and get published in Paris: a cool dissection of the stages and processes of love, that is to say, romantic love. It is a little book which is a more useful guide to the follies of the heart than any I know. It has the wit that is the result of an absolute and unsentimental truthfulness. But this man who had such a talent for tender emotions reported as many failures as victories, and perhaps we should remember that his hero Fabrizio del Dongo (*The Charterhouse of Parma*) shared with other elect souls his belief that the condition of being in love was superior to the cruder pleasures of consummation.

What extremes this man did hold in balance. The extremest was his passion for Napoleon, which characteristic he bestowed on his dashing young heroes Julien Sorel and Fabrizio del Dongo. The idea of Napoleon stood for nobility of soul, courage to defy belittling circum-stances (like Julien Sorel's misfortune of being born a peasant), loathing of the commonplace – like provincial life; it stood for gallantry, beauty, the vision of an eagle rather than the horizons of a titmouse.

We all have friends we must forgive for incomprehensible weak-nesses, such as an insensate and uncritical admiration for, let's say, power-hungry media moguls. Interesting that searching for a contemporary comparison to that horizon-breaker Napoleon, it is financiers that come to mind, not leaders of nations. What present king, general or leader has the glamour of Napoleon? Perhaps we have become too wise to do anything but groan at the news of yet another Great Helmsman? What makes it more inexplicable is that Stendhal was on the Retreat from Moscow; he lived through that ignominious slaughter by disease and the elements. Yet he loved Napoleon, who he insisted was not to blame for the debacle. But if not him, then who? But we are in the presence of an uncritical passion. Stendhal's Napoleon had little to do with the real Napoleon, was more of an idea of glory and magnificence to set against littleness.

Stendhal is one of those figures who provoke questions apparently far from a cause. I am thinking about an account, by a German soldier – as it happens in Hitler's army, the *Gross Deutschland* – who describes unforgivable cruelties in the training of himself and his comrades, causing mutilations and some deaths. 'But we adored him,' cried the soldier of this sadistic general, 'we would have died for him.' Those soldiers who had not already died in Napoleon's armies adored him though he had ruined their lives. We are up against something dark and twisted here: something, it is certain, very ancient. But ambiguous too. Julien Sorel, adoring Napoleon, or rather that crystallisation of a hundred larger-than-life qualities that bore the name Napoleon, survived the destroying mediocrity of a provincial town, a brutal father, persecutions. As many a youngster since, stuck in some God-forsaken backwater, has survived by repeating some barb by a Stendhal character directed towards local stupidity. 'The Directory in Paris, putting on the airs of a well-established sovereign, revealed a total hatred of anything not mediocre.' (Insert your own government, council, helmsman.)

That was when women in their salons could make the fortunes of young men, whether their lovers or not. 'It is possible to make progress in the world only through women,' counselled Stendhal's friendly mentors. Stendhal's heroes owed all the grace and charm in their lives to women and so did he. He did not only worship love, he loved friendship, both without limits, calculation, self-interest. Only generosity of spirit was permissible.

Arriving in Paris, he developed a friendship with a Baron de Lussinge, who shared his frugalities. But as he got rich, he became miserly and patronised Stendhal's poverty. Stendhal did a very French thing: he changed his café so as not to suffer the company of this man he saw as ruined by money. A painful sacrifice, he called it. But he never made things easy for himself. This memoir is full of opportunities for friend-ship, or for advantageous salons, missed. His excessive sensibility, his pride, the high standards of his demands on people, made him solitary. He was already known as a writer, having published works on music and art, but he was not well known. He suffered some savage reviews, which he cushioned by musing that 'one or other of us must be wrong'.

He missed possible love affairs, even when the memory of his Métilde had become 'a tender, profoundly sad ghost, who, by her apparitions, inclined me powerfully to ideas of tenderness, kindness, justice and indulgence.'

This ghost was not always beneficent. His tale of his failure to make it with a girl procured for him is very funny but mostly because he did not see that it was. He was unconcerned, the girl baffled, since she was young and had not experienced this before. His friends were scornful and unkind. For a short time he acquired a reputation for impotence, but as we know from literature and from life, this could – had he used it – have lured women to his bed, because of their instinct to repair the situation.

But he never did play his cards right. It wasn't in him.

It was painful for him to be in Paris which he had known 'as part of Napoleon's Court'. He had made enemies, too. Offered in 1814 the post of food controller of Paris, by the Chief of Police, he refused. The man who accepted became rich in four or five years 'without stealing'. This brevity is Stendhal's immediately recognisable characteristic, as a writer. He reports here on the financial morals of the time in two words.

'...an officer retired on half-pay, decorated at Waterloo, absolutely deprived of wit, and if such a thing is possible, even more of imagination, foolish, but with perfect manners, and *having had so many women that he had become sincere on their subject*.' (My italics.)

Or this, which could be the synopsis for a novel. 'This Mme Lavenelle is as dry as a piece of parchment and in any case has no wit, and above all no *passion*, and it's quite impossible for her to be affected other than by the sturdy thighs of a company of grenadiers parading through the garden of the Tuileries in white kerseymere knickerbockers.' This time the italics are his. To be without passion: Stendhal could not say anything worse. He might laud Paris as an antidote to Grenoble, but he did not like the French, whom he saw as full of artifice, insincerity, and lacking in passion. 'They love money above all things and never sin out of love or hate.' Unlike the Italians, who are frank and natural and honest – with whom he felt at home:

'That government is good, and that government alone, which guarantees the citizen's security on the highways, his equality before the judges, and judges who are reasonably enlightened, as well as a coinage that is not debased, decent roads, and proper protection when abroad.'

We may imagine how this *mot* went down in the drawing-rooms, under the rule of Bourbons, whom he despised, and under whom flourished every kind of jobbery, sleaze, corruption, just as happens today. This definition reaches heights of smiling insolence towards his peers and towards the regime. In Italy he had been suspected of being a spy; I don't see how he could have avoided being in the police files in Paris.

His trip to England was to defeat his low spirits, and to see the plays of Shakespeare, which he read, often, and which he had written about, together with Racine. The absolute contrast must have pleased him. He saw Kean in Othello, and was astonished that in France and in England they used different gestures to express the same emotions; he also was impressed that Kean spoke his words as if thinking of them for the first time.

He was charmed by Richmond. He disliked descriptions of nature, tried to keep his prose unadorned, like a military dispatch, but Richmond tempted him to forget his austerities. There he was, wandering around London, going to the theatre, but he omitted to court that hostess who would have done him the most good. Instead he was taken to a little house where three poor shy girls with chestnut hair – whores – were kind, and had good hearts.

Stendhal loved women, to use that word not as he did in *On Love*, but as a sentiment of general empathy. He had learned understanding of women with his much-loved sister Pauline, who was something of a madcap and rebel (perhaps inspired by her brother's contempt for the ways of society?). She wrote to him of an escapade where she had dressed as a man and gone out to see the sights one evening. He was horrified. His letter to her says everything about the situation of women then. He implored her never to do such a thing again. If she were caught, or even if there were rumours, then no one would marry her, and she would be doomed to a convent or to spinsterhood.

Get yourself a husband at whatever cost, he told her, and then, once married, you can do as you like. Married women are free; unmarried girls slaves.

He was under no illusions about 'the cost'. The husband in *The Red and the Black*, the town mayor Monsieur de Rênal – has there ever been such a description of a boorish, stupid, rough-riding husband? Yet he is not a bad man, certainly desirable as a husband. Women's helplessness in the face of convention has never been written about more tenderly, but what could be more coldly sensible than that letter? In *The Charterhouse of Parma* he merely records, coldly, that a certain society lady had brought her husband as a dowry eight hundred thousand francs, and was allowed by him eighty a month for expenses. No wonder women adored him, though he was not good-looking.

This memoir is incomplete because he was not writing about what was most on his mind, his time with Métilde. He did not want to sully his memories of her. But it could serve as an introduction to the great novels: here is the ore from which he fashioned *The Red and the Black* and *The Charterhouse of Parma*. There is also his autobiography, *La Vie de Henri Brulard* – he used dozens of pseudonyms: his real name was Marie Henri Beyle. That book is less revealing than this little piece, written when he was raw and bleeding. He confesses he found it hard to keep it in chronological order, but that is good: more like what our memories really are, Napoleon and Métilde, Richmond and Racine and poor shy girls with chestnut hair.

It is getting on for two hundred years since he was in Paris, and wrote this, which is like hearing his voice, perhaps speaking in some drawing-room in his beloved Italy, in the company of charming women, one of whom is his mistress, or has been or will be, and their lovers. Husbands are curiously absent, but any there are, are his good friends. Stendhal's heaven, he dreamed of it; alas his fate took him to less kindly places.

– Doris Lessing, 2003

As he delivered his 'Report on the Mode of Execution of the Decree Against the Enemies of the Revolution' to the National Convention on 3rd March 1794, in the late stages of that period of the French Revolution usually known as 'the Terror', Louis de Saint-Just, the austere member of the Comité de Salut Public and the ally of Robespierre, demonstrated to the full the powers of oratory that had made him famous and feared. His icy prowess as a public speaker, and the lapidary quality of his utterances (so concise as to verge on the sibylline, and so extreme in their implications as to make even the 'incorruptible' Robespierre, adjusting his glasses as he addressed the ranks of the Convention, seem vaguely avuncular in comparison), continue to haunt our imaginings of the Revolution. Something he said on that particular occasion has a particularly enigmatic ring: 'Happiness is a new idea in Europe' (*'Le bonheur est une idée neuve en Europe'*). What did he mean?

In some ways, 'happiness' is of course far from being a new idea in Europe: happiness (or *eudaimonia*) is the aim to which all humans tend, according to Aristotle's *Nicomachean Ethics*. The point, however, is how this happiness is defined and where the forum for its realisation is situated. For Aristotle, happiness ('an activity of the soul in accordance with virtue' or 'in accordance with right functioning') tended to be found most securely in intellectual contemplation, and humans were never going to be as happy as god, or the gods, who could devote their entire timeless existences to such contemplation. Catholicism, especially in the figure of Thomas Aquinas, adopted and adapted this view, adding the specifically Christian rider that all earthly happiness was merely a foretaste of the happiness awaiting the blessed in heaven. The eighteenth-century *philosophes* of France, seeing in this deferral of happiness to a post-mortem existence an ideology of renunciation whose pay-off was at best uncertain, began to query why we should not be happy here and now. Heinrich Heine, influenced both by the Enlightenment that spread from these *philosophes* and by his own more specific unrest, expressed the longing for an earthly fulfilment that would be realised in a tangible form, not sequestrated by the powers of this world to the exclusion of those on whose labours their own 'happiness' was predicated. In *Deutschland: ein Wintermärchen* (*Germany: a Winter's Tale*, published in 1844), Heine voiced the sentiments of the so-called 'Young' (or 'Left') Hegelians, including Feuerbach (and, later on, their intellectual descendant Karl Marx), who viewed the postponement of happiness to the hereafter as playing nicely into the hands of the status quo: deferral of fulfilment as deference to the way things were. At the beginning of his poem, Heine, on a visit to his German homeland from his adopted city of Paris, evokes the girl harpist he meets just the other side of the border, singing of 'love and the sorrows of love, sacrifice and renewed acquaintance, up there, in that better world, where all sufferings vanish'. She sings too 'the old song of renunciation, the lullaby-lullay of heaven, with which they' – the ones, as Heine goes on to make clear, who preach water in public but practise wine in secret – 'lull to sleep that great oafish rascal, the People, when it starts to whimper'. And Heine goes on, in lines that mingle childish singsong, simplistic sloganising, and the gravity of the revolutionary demand for bread and justice in the here and now, to insist that 'we want to be happy on earth,' for 'we can leave heaven to the angels and the sparrows.'

This, presumably, was the happiness that for Saint-Just was a 'new idea in Europe': a concrete, active, shared happiness that would not involve extorting yet more 'renunciation' from a populace that – as the series of disastrous failed harvests in the years leading up to the French Revolution showed – faced renunciation every day of its life. Happiness was a new idea in that it had hitherto remained, as far as the *philosophes* were concerned, just that: a mere idea. It is easy, of course, to wax ironical at the word 'happiness' in the mouth of a man whose zeal for revolutionary purity sent so many of his contemporaries to the guillotine, where he himself (together with Robespierre) ended up, aged twenty-seven, only months (28th July) after his speech on happiness. Not for nothing was Saint-Just known as 'the Archangel of the Terror'. It is easy, too, in hindsight, to see how revolutionary aspirations soon degenerated into paranoia and violence, the 'idea' of happiness being confiscated into the service of the age's new idol, the Republic One and Indivisible (or, as it is also known, the modern territorial nation state). But in many ways, the link between happiness and politics remains – problematic but unavoidable.

And this brings us to Stendhal. It may seem a long way from the overheated rhetoric of the National Convention to the jottings of a middle-aged man looking back, a little wistfully, on his life as he whiles away the time in Rome, between official engagements in his capacity as French consul to a minor Italian town in the Papal States (for this is what the *Memoirs of an Egotist* are). But it is happiness that provides the link: happiness and politics. Think of Stendhal, and his sound bites on happiness crowd into the mind: 'beauty is a promise of happiness' (a resolutely unidealistic aesthetic which attracted the admiration of Nietzsche); you can tell what a man is like by seeing how he sets out each morning on his *chasse au bonheur*, his 'pursuit of happiness'; and then there is the ending he gave to his novel *The Charterhouse of Parma*, dedicating the work 'TO THE HAPPY FEW' – a cadence that, coming as it does after the unexpected deaths of almost all the main characters, adds an ironic disjunction to the book's conclusion, suggesting too that, perhaps, the happy are indeed few and far between.

The bits of English, or Frenglish, that dot Stendhal's works, in-cluding the *Memoirs of an Egotist*, are not usually so effective, being part of his habit of, as it were, texting himself in a playful shorthand. There is one occasion in the *Memoirs*, however, where Stendhal's English rises above the jokily illiterate to achieve real poetry and pathos; it is when he goes to visit two pale-faced, doll-like English whores somewhere south of the Thames, and, touched by the neatness of their tiny house and garden, resolves to return the following night with some real champagne, and spends the day looking forward to the evening 'full of snugness' (in English). It does not require much imagination to guess that the life of a whore in early nineteenth-century London was not over-full of 'snugness' (nor, at this point, was Stendhal's); and no doubt the champagne was very welcome; but without wishing to condemn prostitution as such, a political issue it remains, like all intersections of private and public life, and to see this episode as *merely* idyllic (for all the magic with which Stendhal recounts it) would be to falsify and sentimentalise it. But this brings us back to the politics of happiness, and no one was more aware than

Stendhal of the way these two words are inseparable. How could one be happy in the Europe of Metternich? The revolutionary idea seemed dead (discredited by the crimes committed in its name, or simply because it was revolutionary), the wars and alarms of the Napoleonic period were over, reaction had set in, the narrow self-interests of burgeoning capitalism had taken centre stage, politics was *boring*. (*Plus ça change…*) The France of Louis XVIII filled Stendhal with nausea: personal unhappiness may have led him to dally with the Hamletic idea of killing the king (if this is how to decode his cryptic remarks in Stendhalese English). This may have amounted to no more than the slightly crazed fantasies of a Pierre Bezuhov, planning to assassinate Napoleon in Moscow (*War and Peace*), but the amiable Stendhal, that thoroughly modern writer, was also in many respects an old-fashioned Jacobin with a very definite Grand Narrative in view (the overthrowing of tyrants – at least if they were Bourbons); his consular posting to the backwater of Civitavecchia was largely due to the fact that a more desirable posting (to Milan, for instance) had been blocked by the Austrian authorities who then ruled so much of Northern Italy. They had already expelled him from Milan as a potential revolutionary and a sympathiser with the Carbonari in 1821, and the *Memoirs of an Egotist* are shot through with his indignation and pain at being exiled from Milan, the city he loved so much that he planned a tombstone for himself (it is noteworthy that these *Memoirs* centre on such a funereal object) on which he would be described as 'Errico Beyle, Milanese'. His 'real' name, after all, was Henri Beyle, 'Stendhal' was merely the best-known of his many pseudonyms – and again, together with the play-acting that was such an integral part of his character, it may have been politically expedient for someone who never shook off the suspicions of the reactionary authorities dominating the post-1815 European settlement to keep people guessing as to his 'true' identity or 'real' name. (That he succeeded all too well is suggested by the fact that even his liberal friends started to think that such a shape-changer might after all be in the pay of the reactionary governments he seemed to despise.)

And this returns us, ultimately, to the difficulty of any equation linking the two variables 'politics' and 'happiness'. It is true that

Stendhal's most memorable hero, Julien Sorel (in the novel *The Red and the Black*), goes to the guillotine having declared himself to be 'a plebeian… at war with the whole of society'. But he is not in any pure sense a political victim: the reason for his death sentence is that he has tried to shoot the woman he had once loved, Mme de Rênal; and, reconciled to her as he waits in prison for the sentence to be carried out, he discovers that the moments in his life which, retrospectively, fill him with the most happiness were not his achievements in rising (like his hero Bonaparte) from a humble background to a position of power and prestige, but the afternoons spent chasing butterflies in the garden with Mme de Rênal and her children. Call no man happy until he is dead – or: do not imagine you know where the happiness of your life really lay until you are about to die. And the man who placed such a high value on happiness produced, in the *Memoirs*, a text that is haunted by loss. The loss of Napoleon, first, whom Stendhal 'adored', dead in exile on St Helena in 1821; elsewhere he showed a much more nuanced view of the genial despot, but Napoleon was still worth a thousand 'legitimate' kings, and his fall was the pretext for political regression through most of Europe.

Second, and ultimately more important, was the loss of Métilde Dembowski, the love of his life. He had met her in 1818; she was beautiful, haughty and unattainable (though, as so often, we only really have his side of the story); she reduced the outwardly urbane but inwardly hypersensitive Stendhal to trembling gaucherie. He wrote to her, 'I shall love you for the rest of my life; nothing you do will ever change the idea which strikes upon my soul, the idea that I am made for the happiness of being loved by you, or the contempt which this gives me for any other sort of happiness…' Ah, so *that's* what happiness (or the idea of happiness) is – or might have been. Her rejection of Stendhal reduced him to desperate measures, such as pursuing her to Volterra disguised in green spectacles while simultaneously trying to attract her attention by walking casually up and down in the places he knew she would be. She was also viewed as a political subversive by the Austrian authorities; she was to die of consumption in 1825 at the age of thirty-five. Throughout the *Memoirs*, whenever Stendhal mentions 'Italy' he is thinking of Milan, and 'Milan' means 'Métilde'; life in Paris or London is an exile from her, and his unhappiness is so great as to make him fear for his sanity and contemplate suicide. But his unhappiness also made him witty, and brevity is the soul of wit. Which brings us to the fragment – and also to the relationship between happiness and language, a relationship as unstable as that between happiness and politics. Stendhal refers on several occasions to the sheer pleasure he took in writing the *Memoirs*, and the overall tone of *Memoirs of an Egotist* is bright, chirpy, and nonchalant: the work was dashed down in an improvisational style, almost a stream of consciousness or burst of surrealistic automatic writing, begun on 20th June 1832 and stopped in mid-flow, never to be resumed, on 4th July. The sheer brio and zest of the text have a tonic effect. But while the gusto of Stendhal's fragmentary notes, his refusal to be bored, is a way of creating pleasure, we must beware of thinking that it is in itself any mode of truth. A modern prejudice decrees that truth impinges on us from outside, from the Other, in epiphanic moments of being: but these jottings are no more 'authentic' than the sustained, mannered, composed sentences found, for example, in the *Memoirs* of Stendhal's *bête noire*, Chateaubriand. Both Stendhal's allegro vivace and Chateaubriand's andante sostenuto are equally *artificial*, and, in lesser hands, Stendhal's perfunctory and darting shorthand might be less readable, and no more reliable (for all his claims to the contrary) than the echoing vaults of his rival's ornate rhetoric. You can hide in a building site just as much as in a mausoleum. But in any case, Stendhal has a different reason for being elliptical: he is convinced – and this realisation sounds like a refrain from beginning to end of his work – that happiness might be betrayed if you try to write it down. This is one reason for the melancholy that attends the ending of the great novels: the extremes of passion evade transcription in them. The young and handsome and beautiful and talented have their brief and often mute happiness and die, leaving the ugly, middle-aged novelist (or those poignant survivors of *The Charterhouse* and *The Red and the Black*, Mathilde de la Môle and Count Mosca, 'immensely rich', as if *that* made up for anything) to record their fates at length, just as blind old Homer sang of Achilles and Hector. That is what writing is, even at its most fragmentary: a garrulous survivor. It comes too late for extremes of either happiness or unhappiness, and makes up for its belatedness by loquacious invention. Hegel noted that the happy pages in history are all blank, and more recent history has suggested how inexpressible (how unwriteable) the miseries and horrors of that same history may be. Fragments attempt to mimic the disintegration or attenuation of everyday subjectivity attendant on such extreme states: but it is indeed *mere* mimicry – as naive a disguise as wearing green spectacles.

Sometimes, of course, happiness can take refuge in writing itself, so that even writing about unhappiness (as so often in the *Memoirs*) becomes – in a familiar paradox – pleasurable. But there is a negative side to this, as when writing (or 'the aesthetic') becomes the *only* locus of happiness. Saint-Just's maxim is itself then dragged to the guillotine for decapitation: happiness is a new idea. A new idea – one that we have not had before: the effervescence of the sudden insight, the witty bon mot, the moment of understanding, that then passes (or has to be worked out in laborious detail – much less fun). Or a very old idea: the sudden reminiscence that seems to raise us above the contingencies of time and the constraints of teleology (and again seems to deny the labour of transformation that would be involved in bringing the idea to fruition). But an idea, all the same. A 'nice idea'? One, in other words, that never works in practice because to try to realise it would be to betray it, and lead to greater unhappiness than the maintenance of the status quo, however unsatisfactory? No: ideas, however 'regulatory' they may seem, standing aloof above the fray, have a momentum towards their own realisation, even if we are not merely to copy them or treat them as blueprints, for this would be to fall into the illusions of mimicry (and thus mimesis) – Stendhal's happiness, for instance, is not ours: we do not need to share his love of Cimarosa or his detestation of Chateaubriand (happiness is never just a question of taste, of 'I like / I don't like'). The *Memoirs* are not a 'do-it-yourself' manual for happiness. But they may be, together with Stendhal's oeuvre as a whole, as much its organon as Aristotle's *Ethics*. He cannot recapture his happiness in writing, or dictate the terms on which it can be regained, but he can preserve its promise. And not just a permanent promise (the promise of a revelation – or revolution – that does not happen): one that is to be fulfilled, not deferred – as we have seen

Heine emphasising. Stendhal, registering in the *Memoirs* the disastrous impact on the English labouring classes of a combination of the Protestant work ethic and the Industrial Revolution, knew that the eighteenth-century question of happiness was not dead: it had just gone underground, where it was reinventing its strategies. The political system was stagnant, civil society had yet to gain its legitimacy, Europe had failed to throw off its chains. *Plus c'est la même chose, plus ça doit changer*. The angels and sparrows might yet come down to earth: real happiness, like the Good, is a diffusive and communicative power. How powerfully (if indirectly) Stendhal communicates it! – and thus ceases to be a mere egotist. Having beheaded one of Saint-Just's aphorisms, let us end with another, as oracular and enigmatic as the first in its yoking of happiness with politics: '*Les malheureux sont les puissances de la terre*': 'the wretched (or, quite simply, the unhappy) are the powers (and the potentialities) of the earth'.

– *Andrew Brown, 2003*

Note on the Text:

This translation is based on Stendhal, *Souvenirs d'Egotisme*, ed. Béatrice Didier (Paris: Gallimard, 'Folio', 1983). The quotation from Stendhal's letter to Métilde is taken from the fine biography by Jonathan Keates, *Stendhal* (London: Sinclair-Stevenson, 1994), pp. 231–2.

Memoirs of an Egotist

MEMOIRS

I leave this analysis to M. Abraham Constantin, the famous painter, asking him to give it to some printer devoid of bigotry, ten years after me, or to have it deposited in some library if no one is prepared to print it. B[envenut]o Cellini was published fifty years after his death.

– H. Beyle

Begun on the 20th June driven like the Pythian oracle. Continued on the 21st after the procession. Tired.

Table of contents

[Codicil to the holograph will of M. Henri Beyle, French consul at Civitavecchia.]

Civitavecchia, 24th June 1832

I, the undersigned, H.-M. Beyle, leave the present manuscript containing ramblings on my private life to M. Abraham Constantin of Geneva, the famous painter, chevalier of the Legion of Honour, etc., etc. I ask M. A. Constantin to have this manuscript printed ten years after my death. I ask him to change nothing; however, the names can be changed and imaginary names substituted for the ones I have set down; for example print Mme Durand or Mme Delpierre instead of Mme Doligny or Mme Berthois.

H. Beyle

I would quite like all the names to be changed. The real ones could be substituted if by chance these ramblings are reprinted fifty years after my death.

H. Beyle

Memoirs of an Egotist

Not to be printed until ten years after my decease, out of consideration for the persons named, even though two thirds of them are already dead anyway.

CHAPTER ONE*

So as to make some use of my leisure periods in this foreign country, I feel like writing a short memoir of what happened to me during my last trip to Paris, from 21st June 1821 to ** November 1830. It's a space of nine and a half years. I've been scolding myself for two months, since I absorbed the novelty of my position, urging myself to do some work. Without work, the ship of human life has no ballast. I confess that I wouldn't have any motive for writing if I didn't imagine that one day these pages will be printed, and read by someone I love, a person such as Mme Roland or M. Gros, the geometrician. But the eyes that will read this are barely opening to the light of day, I estimate that my future readers are ten or twelve years old.

Have I derived the maximum benefit and the greatest happiness from the positions in which chance has placed me during the nine years I have just spent in Paris? What kind of man am I? Do I have common sense, do I have common sense and profundity too?

Am I remarkably witty? Truth to tell, I haven't the slightest idea. I'm affected by what happens to me day by day, I rarely think about these fundamental questions, and then my judgements vary with my mood. My judgements are merely off-the-cuff comments.

Let's see whether, examining my conscience with pen in hand, I will reach any *positive* conclusion that will remain *true* in my eyes *for a long time*. What will I think about the things I feel inclined to write when I reread them around 1835, if I live? Will it be the same as for my published works? I have a deep sense of sadness when, not having any other book, I reread them.

I feel, thinking over it for the past month, a real disgust at the idea of writing merely in order to talk about myself, how many shirts I have, everything that has affected my self-esteem. On the other hand, I am far away from France**; I've read all the entertaining books that have managed to find their way into this country. My wholehearted

* 21 pages 20th June 1832, Mero[1].
** He was then cons[ul] of France in the Roman States and resident at C[ivita]v[ecchi]a and Mero.

inclination was to write a work of fiction based on a love affair that happened in Dresden, in August 1813, in a house next door to mine, but the routine duties of my job interrupt me quite frequently, or, more precisely, I can never be sure when I pick up my piece of paper that I'll be able to spend an hour without being interrupted. This minor irritation completely puts a damper on my imagination. When I get back to my fiction, I find what I was thinking quite repellent. To which a wise man will reply that we have to conquer ourselves. My answer will be: it's too late, I'm 4[9] years old; after so many adventures, it's time to start thinking of getting to the end of life as painlessly as possible.

My principal objection wasn't the *vanity* involved in writing one's life story. A book on such a subject is like all the others; you soon forget it if it's boring. I was afraid of deflowering the happy moments that I encountered if I described them or anatomised them. Well that's just what I won't do, I'll skip over the periods of happiness.

Poetic genius is dead, but the genius of *suspicion* has come into the world. I'm profoundly convinced that the only antidote that can make the reader forget the perpetual *I*'s the author will be writing, is a perfect sincerity. Will I be brave enough to narrate humiliating events without making excuses for them in endless prefaces? I hope so.

Despite the disappointments that my ambition met with, I don't think men are wicked; I don't think I am persecuted by them, I regard them as machines impelled, in France, by *vanity* and, elsewhere, by all the passions, vanity included.

I do not know myself and this is what sometimes, at night-time when I think about it, upsets me. Am I good, bad, clever, stupid? Have I managed to derive the maximum benefit from the chance events into which I was flung both by the omnipotence of Napoleon (whom I always adored) in 1810, and by the way we fell into the mire in 1814, and our effort to crawl out of it in 1830? I'm afraid the answer is no, I acted on impulse, at random. If anyone had asked me for advice about my own position, I would often have given weighty advice: friends of mine who are rivals in wit have complimented me on the fact.

In 1814, Count Beugnot, Minister of Police, offered me a post organising the food provisions for Paris. I wasn't angling for a post, I was in an admirable position to accept, I replied in such a way as to give no encouragement to M. Beugnot, a man who has enough vanity for two Frenchmen; he must have been quite shocked. The man who got this job retired after four or five years, tired of earning money and doing so – it is said – without stealing. The extreme contempt I had for the Bourbons, it was at the time a fetid mire for me, made me leave Paris a few days after not accepting M. Beugnot's kind offer. My heart was broken by the triumph of everything I held in contempt but was unable to hate, and it was revived only by my first faint stirrings of love for Countess du Long, whom I met every day at M. Beugnot's and who, ten years later, played a great part in my life. At the time she picked me out, not as being likeable, but as eccentric. She saw me as the friend of a really ugly woman of great character: Countess Beugnot. I've always regretted the fact I didn't love her. What a pleasure it must be to talk intimately to a person of such far-reaching ideas!

This preface is pretty long, I've felt as much for three pages. But I have to begin with a subject so sad and difficult that inertia is already overwhelming me; I almost feel like throwing down my pen. But the minute I found myself feeling lonely, I would regret it.

I left Milan for Paris on the ** June 1821, with a sum of 3,500 francs, I think, and convinced that my sole happiness lay in blowing my brains out when I'd run through this sum. I was leaving, after three years of intimacy, a woman whom I adored, who loved me and who never gave herself to me. I am still after so many intervening years trying to work out the reasons behind her behaviour. She had been deeply dishonoured, and yet she had only ever had one lover, but the high-society women of Milan took revenge for her superiority. Poor Métilde[2] never managed to manoeuvre against this enemy, nor to treat it with contempt. Perhaps one day, when I am an old man whose passions have cooled, I will have the strength to talk about the years 1818, 1819, 1820, 1821.

In 1821, I found it very difficult indeed to resist the temptation of blowing my brains out. I drew a pistol in the margin of a mediocre love drama I was scribbling at the time (staying in the Casa Acerbi). It seems to me that it was political curiosity that stopped me ending it all; perhaps, without my suspecting it, I was also afraid of hurting myself.

Finally I took my leave of Métilde. – 'When will you return?' she said to me. – 'Never, I hope.' Then there was a final hour of desultory exchanges and vain words; a single word could have changed my future life, alas! not for very long, that angelic soul concealed within such a beautiful body departed this life in 1825.

Finally, I left in a state one can easily imagine on the ** June. I travelled from Milan to Como, fearing and indeed believing at every moment that I would turn back.

'I had thought I would not be able to stay in that town without dying, but I was unable to leave it without a terrible wrench to my soul; it seemed to me that I was leaving behind my life; indeed, what was life compared to her (Métilde)? I expired at every step I took away from it. Every breath was a sigh' – Shelley[3].*

Soon I was in a kind of stupor, making conversation with the postilions and replying perfectly seriously to these people's opinions of the price of wine. I weighed up with them all the reasons for raising the price by a sou; the most dreadful thing was to turn my thoughts inwards. I came to Airolo, Bellinzona, Lugano (the sound of these names still makes me shudder even today, 20th June 1832).

I reached the Saint-Gothard – at the time an abominable pass (exactly like the mountains of Cumberland in the north of England, but with precipices too). I wanted to travel through the Saint-Gothard pass on horseback, vaguely hoping that I'd fall off and get badly grazed, which would take my mind off things. Although I'm an ex-cavalry officer, and although I've spent my life falling off horses, I hate falling on scree when the stones give way beneath the horse's hooves.

The courier I was with finally stopped me and said he couldn't care less whether I got killed, but that I'd cut down his profit, and nobody would want to come with him when they found out that one of his travellers had tumbled down the precipice.

'So haven't you guessed I've got the c***?[4]' I told him. 'I can't walk.'

I finally arrived: the courier continued to grumble at his fate all the way to Altorf. I gazed in astonishment at everything I saw. I'm a great admirer of William Tell, although the ministerial writers of every country pretend he never existed. In Altorf, I think it was, a bad statue of Tell with a stone skirt touched me precisely because it was so bad.

* Indent the quotation.

'So,' I said to myself, with a sweet melancholy, giving way for the first time to a dry-eyed despair, 'so that is what happens to the most beautiful things in the eyes of coarse men! That is what happens to you, Métilde, in the salon of Mme Traversi!'

The sight of this statue soothed me a little. I asked where Tell's chapel could be found. – 'You can see it tomorrow.'

The next day, I embarked in quite awful company: Swiss officers comprising part of the guard of Louis XVIII, who were making their way to Paris.

(Here four pages of descriptions of the journey from Altorf to Gersau, Lucerne, Basel, Belfort, Langres, Paris. I prefer to concentrate on spiritual things, describing physical things bores me. It's been two years since I've written twelve pages like this.)

I have never liked France, the outskirts of Paris in particular, which proves that I'm a bad Frenchman and a wicked individual, Mlle Sophie would later say… (M. Cuvier's daughter-in-law). My heart contracted painfully on the journey between Basel and Belfort as I left behind the high if not beautiful Swiss mountains for the dreadful flat wastes of Champagne. How ugly the women are in ***, a village where I saw them wearing blue stockings and wooden shoes. But later on I said to myself: 'What politeness, what affability, what a sense of justice in the conversation of those villagers!'

The physical situation of Langres resembled that of Volterra, a town I adored at the time. It had been the scene* of one of my boldest exploits in my war against Métilde.

I thought of Diderot (who was, as everyone knows, the son of a Langres cutler), I thought of *Jacques the Fatalist*, the only one of his works I admire, but I admire it much more than I do the *Voyage d'Anarchasis*, the *Traité des Etudes*, and a hundred such tomes admired by all the pedants.[5]

'The worst of all misfortunes,' I exclaimed, 'would be for those unemotional men, my friends, in whose company I am going to live, to find out about my passion, and for a woman I never had!'

I said this to myself in June 1821, and I see in June 1832, for the first time, as I write this, that this fear, repeated a thousand times over, has in

* 20th June 1832, 15 pages in 1 hour.

fact been the governing principle of my life for ten years. It's the reason why I became so *witty*, something that was… the *block*, the butt of my scorn in Milan in 1818 when I was in love with Métilde.

I entered Paris, which I found worse than ugly, a real insult to my suffering, with a single idea in my head: *not to be found out*. After a week, seeing the political vacuum I told myself, '[Must] take advantage of my suffering to k L 18[6].'

I lived off that hope for several months which I can barely remember. I bombarded my friends in Milan with letters to get from them indirectly even a scrap of information about Métilde, though they disapproved of my foolishness and never spoke about it.

I took lodgings in Paris, in the rue de Richelieu, in the Hôtel de Bruxelles, No. 47, run by a M. Petit, a former manservant of one of the MM. de Damas. This M. Petit's politeness, his grace, his knack of saying the right thing, his absence of all feeling, his horror of any movements of the soul with any depth to them, his vivid memory for things that had flattered his vanity thirty years before, his perfect sense of honour when it came to money, all made him in my eyes the perfect model of an old-style Frenchman. I soon entrusted him with the three thousand francs still remaining to me, and despite my objections he handed me a receipt chit that I rapidly lost, which vexed him greatly when, a few months after or a few weeks, I took my money back from him to go to England where I was impelled to go by the deadly disgust I felt for Paris.

I have very few memories of those passionate times, things slid over me unnoticed or viewed with contempt when I did take vague notice of them. My thoughts were on Belgiojoso Square in Milan. I'm going to summon my strength to try and remember the houses I visited.*

---

* 20th June 1832. My hand's tired, it's the 18th page.

CHAPTER TWO

Here is the portrait of a man of merit with whom I spent all my mornings for eight years. There was esteem, but no friendship.

I'd taken lodgings at the Hôtel de Bruxelles, because also living there was the most unemotional, harshest Piedmontese, the man most resembling the figure of Rancour (in the *Roman comique*) that I have ever encountered.[7] The Baron de Lussinge was my life's companion from 1821 to 1831; born in about 1785, he was thirty-six in 1821. He started to detach himself from me and become impolite in conversation when I gained a reputation for wittiness, after the terrible disaster of 15th September 1826[8].

M. de Lussinge, short, broad-shouldered, thick-set, unable to see more than three steps ahead, always shabbily dressed out of avarice, and using our walks together to draw up budgets of personal expenditure, had, for a chap living alone in Paris, an unusual sagacity. In my romantic and brilliant illusions, I would give a mark of thirty to the genius, the kindness, the fame, the happiness of a man passing by, when he only deserved fifteen; my companion gave him only six or seven.

This is what formed the basis of our conversations for eight years, we would seek each other out the length and breadth of Paris.

Lussinge, aged thirty-six or thirty-seven at the time, had the head and the heart of a man of fifty-five*. The only thing that affected him deeply was events personal to him; then he'd go out of his mind, as at the time of his marriage. Apart from that, the constant butt of his irony was emotion. Lussinge had only one religion: the esteem in which he held high birth; he himself comes from a family in the Bugey; they held an elevated rank there in 1500; they followed to Turin the dukes of Savoy, who later became kings of Sardinia. Lussinge had been educated in Turin at the same academy as Alfieri[9]; there he had imbibed that deep Piedmontese malice, unparalleled anywhere else in the world, which is, however, merely a mistrust of men and destiny. I come across several of the same characteristics here in Emor; but here, into the bargain, there are passions, and as things are played out on a wider stage, there's less bourgeois pettiness. For all that, I liked Lussinge until

---

* Tired by these 21 pages, 20th June 1832.

13

he became rich, and then avaricious, timid and eventually disagreeable in his remarks and almost uncivil in January 1830.

He had a mother who was avaricious but above all quite mad, and capable of giving away all her wealth to the priests. He thought of marrying; it would be an opportunity for his mother to contract obligations that would prevent her from giving her wealth away to her confessor. The different intrigues and the steps he took when he went out wife-hunting gave us a great deal of amusement. Lussinge was on the point of asking for the hand of a charming girl who would have given happiness to him and eternity to our friendship: I mean the daughter of G[ener]al Gilly (who has since become Mme Doin, the wife of a solicitor, I believe). But the general had been condemned to death after 1815, something that would have frightened away the noble Baroness, Lussinge's mother. By great good fortune, he escaped marrying a coquette, who has since become Mme Varambon. Finally, he married a perfect ninny, tall and quite attractive, if only she'd had a decent nose. This ninny took as her confessor M. de Quélen himself, the Archbishop of Paris, in whose salon she would go to make her confession. Chance had given me some information about the love affairs of this Archbishop who was at the time involved with Mme de Podenas, the lady-in-waiting of the Duchess de Berry, and, since or before that time, mistress of the all-too-famous Duke de Raguse. One day, indiscreetly for me – and this is, if I'm not mistaken, one of my numerous failings – I teased Mme de Lussinge a bit about the Archbishop. It was in the home of the Countess d'Avelles. 'Cousin, get M. Beyle to shut up!' she cried in a rage.

Ever since, she has been my enemy, though with renewed outbreaks of the strangest flirtatiousness. But here I find myself embarked on a very long episode; I'll keep going, as I saw Lussinge twice a day for eight years, and later on I ought to return to this grand and flourishing Baroness who is almost five foot six.

With his dowry, his salary as head clerk in the Ministry of Police, the money he got from his mother, Lussinge's income amounted to twenty-two or twenty-three livres around 1828. From this time on, a single sentiment dominated his life: the fear of losing. Despising the Bourbons, not as much as I who am politically virtuous, but despising them for being clumsy, he came to the point where he could no longer tolerate without a violent fit of ill temper any expression of their blunders. (He saw with great clarity the possibility of some danger to his property suddenly looming.) Every day he received news of them, as can be seen from the newspapers between 1826 and 1830. Lussinge would go to the theatre in the evenings, and never out into society, he felt a little humiliated by his position. Every morning, we would meet up in the café; I told him what I'd learnt the evening before; usually we would joke about our different party allegiances. On 3rd January 1830, I think it was, he denied some anti-Bourbon comment I had heard at the home of M. Cuvier, at the time a Councillor of State, a really ministerial character[10]. This foolish remark was followed by a very long silence; we crossed the Louvre without speaking. At the time I had only the strict minimum of money; he, as I've said, had twenty-two thousand francs. I thought I'd noticed, over the past year, that he'd been starting to adopt a tone of superiority towards me. In our political discussions, he told me, '*You* don't have a fortune.'

Finally I decided to make the painful sacrifice of changing café without telling him. I'd been going for nine years every day at half-past ten to the Café de Rouen, run by M. Pique, a nice middle-class fellow, and Mme Pique, a pretty woman in those days, from whom Maisonnette, one of the friends we had in common, obtained, I believe, assignations at 500 francs a time. I withdrew from Café Lemblin, the well-known liberal café, also situated in the Palais-Royal.* Now I saw Lussinge only once a fortnight; since that time, our intimacy, which for both of us had become, I think, a need, has often attempted to renew itself, but it's never been strong enough to do so. On several later occasions, music or painting, on which he was well-informed, constituted neutral terrain for us, but the complete lack of politeness in his manners returned in all its harshness the minute we started talking politics and he grew afraid for his twenty-two thousand francs; there was no way of continuing. His common sense prevented me from getting too lost in my poetic illusions. My cheerfulness, for I became cheerful or rather I acquired the art of appearing so, distracted him from his gloomy, malicious temper and from the dreadful *fear of losing*.

* 21st June [1832]

15

When I managed to get a minor job back, in 1830, I think he found the salary too high. But anyway, between 1821 and 1828 I saw Lussinge twice a day, and apart from love and my literary plans which he understood nothing about, we chatted at length about each of my actions, in the Tuileries and on the quai du Louvre which led to his office. From eleven in the morning until half-past twelve we were together and, as often as not, he managed to take my mind completely off my sorrows of which he knew nothing.

Well, that's the end of that long episode, but it was a question of introducing the first character in these memoirs, the man whom, later on, I injected in such an amusing fashion with my frenzied love of Mme Azur whose faithful lover he has since been for the last two years and, what is even more comical, he has made *her* faithful. She is one of the least *doll-like* Frenchwomen I have ever met.

But let's not get ahead of ourselves. Nothing is more difficult in this solemn narrative than respecting chronological order.

So, we'd got as far as August 1821, and I was lodging with Lussinge at the Hôtel de Bruxelles, following him at five o'clock to the excellent table d'hôte kept by the most polite of Frenchmen, M. Petit, and by his wife, a chambermaid in the grand style, but still crack-brained. There, Lussinge who was always afraid – as I now see in 1832 – to introduce me to his friends, couldn't stop himself from getting me to meet:

1. a likeable, excellent fellow, handsome but devoid of wit, M. Barot, a banker from Charleville, then busy gaining a fortune of eighty thousand francs' annual income;
2. an officer retired on half-pay, decorated at Waterloo, absolutely deprived of wit, and if such a thing is possible, even more of imagination, foolish, but with perfect manners, and having had so many women that he had become sincere on their subject.

The conversation of M. Poitevin, the sight of his common sense absolutely free of any exaggeration due to imagination, his ideas on women, his advice on clothes, were all of great use to me. I think this poor Poitevin had a fixed income of 1,200 francs and a job that brought in 1,500 francs. On top of that, he was one of the best-dressed young men in Paris. Admittedly, he never went out without spending two hours getting ready – sometimes two and a half. Anyway, he'd had a brief fling for two months, I think, with the Marquise de Rosine to whom later on I was so deeply obliged that I promised myself ten times over I would have her. Which I never tried to do, and I was wrong. She forgave me my ugliness and I really owed it to her to become her lover. I'll try and pay off this debt on my first trip to Paris; maybe she will be all the more susceptible to my attentions now that neither of us is still young. Moreover, perhaps I am being too boastful, she's really behaved herself over the last ten years, but in my view it's because she has no choice.

Finally, being abandoned by Mme Dar. on whom I was inevitably counting so much, I owe the Marquise the most heartfelt thanks.

It's only as I mull over it all so as to write it down that what was happening in my heart in 1821 starts to become clearer to my eyes. I've always lived, and still do, from day to day, and without thinking in the slightest of what I'll do tomorrow. Time's progress is marked for me only by Sundays, when I usually get bored and find everything hard to take. I've never been able to decide why. In 1821, in Paris, the Sundays were really horrible for me. All alone under the spreading chestnut trees of the Tuileries, so majestic at that time of year, I thought of Métilde, who would spend those days in particular at the home of the opulent Mme Traversi. That fateful friend, who hated me, was jealous of her cousin and had persuaded her, through her and through her friends, that she would dishonour herself entirely if she took me as a lover. Absorbed in sombre daydreams all the time I wasn't with my three friends, Lussinge, Barot and Poitevin, I would accept their company only as a way of taking my mind off things. The pleasure of being distracted for a moment from my pain, or my extreme reluctance to be distracted from it, dictated all I did. When one of those Messieurs suspected me of being downcast, I would talk a lot, and I would sometimes say the most foolish things, and those things that you should never say especially in France, because they offend the vanity of the person you are talking to. M. Poitevin made me suffer a hundredfold for those remarks.

I've always talked much too much at random and without much caution; in those days, talking only to assuage for an instant a piercing pain, and with the intention above all of avoiding the reproach of having left behind a loved one in Milan and being downcast for that reason, which would have brought down on my supposed mistress jocular comments that I would not have tolerated – I must really have appeared, to those three persons perfectly devoid of imagination, completely mad. I found out a few years later that they had simply thought me extremely affected. I see as I write this that if chance, or a little prudence, had impelled me to seek the company of women, in spite of my age, my ugliness, etc., I would have been successful with them and perhaps found some consolation. I had a mistress only by chance in 1824, three years later. Only then did the memory of Métilde cease to be such a wrench. She became for me a tender, profoundly sad ghost, who, by her apparitions, inclined me powerfully to ideas of tenderness, kindness, justice and indulgence.

It was a real chore for me in 1821 to return for the first time to the houses in which people had shown me kindness when I was attached to Napoleon's Court (*There*[11], the details of those circles). I kept putting it off, leaving it for later. Finally, as I had after all had to greet the friends I met in the streets, my presence in Paris became common knowledge, and they complained of my negligence.

The Count d'Argout, a friend and colleague when we were auditors at the Council of State, a fine fellow, a relentless hard worker, but not at all witty, was a peer of the realm in 1821; he gave me a ticket for the Chamber of Peers, where they were examining the case of a number of silly asses who had acted imprudently and without any logic.[12] Their affair was called, I think, the conspiracy of the 19th or 29th August. It was mere chance that they didn't lose their heads. There it was that I saw for the first time M. Odilon Barrot, a short man with a blue beard. He was defending, as a solicitor, one of those poor idiots who get involved in conspiracy when they have only two thirds or three quarters of the courage needed for such a preposterous action.* I was struck by M. Odilon Barrot's logic. I would usually stand behind the seat of the chancellor M. Dambray, one or two steps away. Here description A´. It seems to me that he conducted all these debates with reasonable decency, for a noble. Here a description of the Chamber of Peers. He had the tone and manners of M. Petit, the proprietor of the Hôtel de

* 21st June

18

Bruxelles, former manservant of M. Damas, but with this difference, that M. Dambray had less noble manners. The next day, I sang the praises of his decency at the home of Countess Doligny. M. d'Ambray's mistress happened to be there, a plump woman of thirty-six, very fresh; she had the ease and figure of Mlle Contat in her last years. (She was an inimitable actress; I'd been a great devotee in 1803, I believe.)

I was wrong not to have an affair with this mistress of M. Dambray, my madness had made me seem distinguished to her eyes. Moreover, she thought I was the lover or one of the lovers of Mme Doligny. There I would have found a remedy for my sorrows, but I was blind.

One day I encountered, coming out of the Chamber of Peers, my cousin, Baron Martial Daru. He was proud of his title; in other ways the best fellow in the world, my benefactor, the master who had taught me, in Milan in 1800 and in Brunswick in 1807, the little I know of the art of behaving towards women. He had twenty-two of them in his life, some of the prettiest around, inevitably the best to be found wherever he was. I've burnt the portraits, locks of hair, letters, etc.

'Well well, you're in Paris! How long have you been here?' – 'Three days.' – 'Come along tomorrow. My brother will be really pleased to see you…' What was my reply to this most amiable and most amicable welcome? I went to see these excellent relatives only six or eight years later. And the shame I felt at not having put in an appearance at the home of my benefactors meant that I went there fewer than ten times before their premature death. Around 1829 the amiable Martial Daru died; he had become coarse and insignificant because of the aphrodisiac potions he took, a subject on which I quarrelled with him two or three times. A few months later, I was thunderstruck in my Café de Rouen, in those days at the corner of the rue du Rempart, to come across the news in my paper announcing the death of Count Daru. I leapt into a cab, tears in my eyes, and hurried over to No. 81 in the rue de Grenelle. I found a footman weeping, and I burst into floods of tears. I felt how ungrateful I'd been; I took my ingratitude to new heights by leaving that very same evening for Italy, I think; I brought my departure forward; I would have died of sorrow if I'd set foot in his house. Here too there was a trace of the madness that made me so baroque in 1821.

M. Doligny junior was also defending one of the wretched fat-heads who had been involved in the conspiracy. From the place he occupied as a solicitor, he saw me; there was no way I could get out of going to see his mother. She had great strength of character, she was a woman, I don't know why I didn't take advantage of the admirable obligingness of her welcome to relate my sorrows to her and ask for her advice. There too I was so close to happiness, for reason, heard from a woman's mouth, would have had quite a different influence over me from any influence I had over myself. I often dined at the home of Mme Doligny; at the second or third dinner she invited me to lunch with the mistress of M. Dambray who was then chancellor. I was a success and I was foolish enough not to immerse myself in that friendly company; accepted as a lover or spurned, I would have found a little of that *oblivion* that I sought everywhere and for instance on my long solitary walks through Montmartre* or the Bois de Boulogne. I was so unhappy there that ever since I have been quite averse to those pleasant spots. But I was blind then. It was only in 1824 when chance gave me a mistress that I saw the remedy to my sorrows.

What I'm writing seems really boring; if it goes on the same way, this won't be a book, but an examination of conscience. I have almost no distinct memories of those times of storm and passion.

The daily sight of my conspirators at the Chamber of Peers struck me deeply with this idea: k[illing] someone you've never spoken to is merely an ordinary duel. How was it that none of those ninnies had the idea of imitating L[ouve]l?[13]

My ideas are so vague on that period of my life that I don't really know if it was in 1821 or 1814 that I met the mistress of M. d'Ambray at the home of Mme Doligny.

It seems to me that in 1821 I saw M. Doligny only at his château in Corbeil, and even then I resolved to go there only after two or three invitations.

* 21st June [1832].

CHAPTER THREE

Love* gave me, in 1821, a thoroughly comic virtue: chastity.

Despite my efforts, in August 1821, MM. Lussinge, Barot, Poitevin, finding me care-worn, arranged a delightful little orgy. Barot, as I have since realised, was one of the most talented people in Paris when it came to this rather tricky kind of pleasure. A woman is a woman for him only once: the first time. He spends thirty thousand of his eighty thousand francs, and, of those thirty thousand francs, at least twenty thousand on whores.

So Barot arranged an evening party with Mme Petit, one of his ex-mistresses to whom he had, I think, just lent some money so as to set up an establishment (*to raise a brothel*[14]), in the rue du Cadran, on the corner of the rue Montmartre, on the fourth floor.

We were to have Alexandrine, who six months later was being kept by the wealthiest Englishmen, but at the time was a beginner with two months' experience. We found, on the stroke of 8 p.m., a charming salon, albeit on the fourth floor, iced champagne, hot punch… Finally Alexandrine appeared, led in by a chambermaid whose job it was to keep an eye on her. Who had given her that job? I've forgotten. But this woman must have had considerable authority, for I saw from the party bill that they had given her twenty francs. Alexandrine appeared and surpassed our expectations. She was a tall, slim girl, seventeen to eighteen years old, already physically mature, with black eyes that I have since found again in the portrait of the Duchess of Urbino by Titian in the Florence gallery. Apart from the colour of her hair, it was *her* portrait that Titian had painted. She was gentle, not at all shy, quite cheerful, well-mannered. My colleagues' eyes almost started from their heads at the sight of her. Lussinge offered her a glass of champagne that she refused, and went off with her. Mme Petit introduced us to two other girls, they were not bad; we told her that she was prettier than them. She had a charming foot. Poitevin took off with her. After a dreadfully long time, Lussinge returned, his face pale.

'Your turn, Belle[15]. All honour to the new arrival!' they all cried. I found Alexandrine lying on a bed, a little tired, almost in the costume

* 21st June.

21

and exactly in the pose of Titian's *Duchess of Urbino*. 'Let's just have a bit of a chat for ten minutes,' she said to me, with great presence of mind. 'I'm rather tired, let's just talk. I'll soon rediscover all the fire of youth.'

She was adorable; I've perhaps never seen a prettier creature. She did not really have the air of a libertine, except in her eyes, which little by little started to sparkle again with wild desire, and, so to speak, pleasure.

I totally botched the job, a complete *fiasco*. I resorted to a compensatory manoeuvre, she was happy to go along. Unsure what to do, I tried to finish the job with my hand again, but she refused. She seemed astonished, I said a few words appropriate enough for my position, and I left.

Hardly had Barot succeeded me than we heard guffaws of laughter coming through three rooms to where we were. All at once Mme Petit dismissed the other girls and Barot led Alexandrine to us:

> …in the apparel bare
> Of a beautiful woman who's just been roused from sleep.[16]

'My admiration for Belle,' he said bursting out laughing, 'means I'm going to imitate him. I've come to fortify myself with champagne.' The explosion of mirth lasted for twenty minutes; Poitevin was rolling on the carpet. The innocent surprise shown by Alexandrine was priceless; it was the first time in her life that anyone had failed with her.

Those gentleman tried to convince me that I was dying of shame and that this was the unhappiest moment in my life. I was surprised, that's all. I don't know why the idea of Métilde had come forcibly to my mind as I entered the room which Alexandrine adorned in such a pretty fashion.

Anyway, for ten years I didn't go with whores more than two or three times. And the first time after the charming Alexandrine was in October or November 1826, being, as I then was, on the point of despair.

I met Alexandrine ten times in the brilliant retinue surrounding her a month later, and I always had a twinge of regret. Eventually, after five or six years, she turned coarse-faced, like her friends.

From that moment on, the three life companions that chance had given me considered me to be a real Babillan[17]. This fine reputation spread through society and to a greater or lesser degree survived until Mme Azur gave an account of my exploits. This party greatly strengthened my friendship with Barot; I still like him and he likes me. He's perhaps the only Frenchman in whose château I would enjoy spending a fortnight. He is the man with the most sincere heart, the firmest character, the least wit and the least education that I know. But in his two talents: that of earning money, without ever gambling at the Stock Exchange, and that of striking up acquaintance with a woman he sees when out for a stroll or at the theatre, he is without an equal, especially in the latter domain.

It's because it's a necessity for him. Any woman who has granted him her favours becomes no different from a man.

One evening, Métilde was telling me about Mme Bignami, her friend. She related of her own accord a quite well-known love story, then added: 'You can judge her fate: every evening her lover, on leaving her apartment, would go off to see a whore.'

Now when I had left Milan, I realised that these moral words had absolutely nothing to do with Mme Bignami's story, but constituted a moral warning for my benefit.

And indeed, each evening, having seen Métilde as far as the house of her cousin, Mme Traversi, to whom I had tactlessly refused to be introduced, I would go off to finish the evening at the home of the charming and divine Countess Kassera. And, through another stupid mistake, closely akin to the one I made with Alexandrine, I refused on one occasion to be the lover of that young woman, the most likeable perhaps that I have ever known; all this so that I could deserve, in God's eyes, the love of Métilde. I refused, in the same spirit and for the same reason, the celebrated Viganò, who one day, as her entire court was descending the stairs – and among the courtiers was that witty man the Count de Saurau – let everyone go past to tell me, 'Belle, they tell me that you're in love with me.' – 'They are wrong,' I replied with great composure, without even kissing her hand. This unworthy action, shown to a woman who was independent and high-spirited, drew down on me her implacable hatred. She no longer even greeted me when, in one of those narrow streets in Milan, we bumped into one another.

Those are three stupid mistakes. I'll never forgive myself for Countess Kassera (these days, she's the most modest and respected woman in the country).

CHAPTER [FOUR]

Here is another circle of acquaintances, contrasting with that of the preceding chapter. In 1817, the man I admired most for his writings, the only one who brought about a revolution within me, Count de Tracy[18], came to see me at the Hôtel d'Italie, place Favart. Never have I been more surprised. For twelve years I had adored this man's *Ideology* which will one day be famous. Someone had left at his home a copy of my *History of Painting in Italy*.

He spent an hour with me. I admired him so much that I probably had a *fiasco* out of excessive love. Never was I less intent on trying to be witty or being agreeable. I came up close to that vast intelligence, and contemplated it in astonishment; I asked him for enlightenment. In any case, in those days, I still was incapable of *being witty*. That way of improvising with a tranquil mind only came to me in 1827.

M. Destutt de Tracy, peer of the realm, member of the Academy, was an old man, short in stature, remarkably dapper and elegant if somewhat eccentric in manner. He usually wears a green visor on the pretext that he is blind. I'd seen him being received into the Academy by M. de Ségur, who said stupid things to him in the name of imperial despotism; it was in 1811, I think. Although attached to the Court, I found it profoundly distasteful. We're going to relapse into military barbarism, we're all going to become like General Gross, I told myself. This general, whom I saw at the home of Countess Daru, was one of the most stupid swordsmen in the Imperial Guard, and that's saying a great deal. He had a Provençal accent, and his most burning ambition was to cut down with his sword all the Frenchmen who were the enemies of the man who provided him with his fodder. This type of character has become my *bête noire*, so much so that on the evening of the Battle of the Moskva, seeing a few paces away from me the remains of two or three generals of the Imperial Guard, I couldn't help remarking, '*that's got rid of a couple of those insolent dogs!*', a comment that almost did for me, and one that in any case was inhumane.

M. de Tracy has never allowed anyone to paint his portrait. I find he resembles Pope Corsini, Clement ***, as he appears at Santa Maria Maggiore in the fine chapel on the left-hand side as you go in.

His manners are perfect when he is not in thrall to an abominable black mood. I never guessed he had such a personality until 1822. He's an old Don Juan (see Mozart's opera, Molière, etc.). Everything throws him into a mood. For instance, in his salon, M. de La Fayette[19] was more of a great man than he was (even in 1821). And then, the French have never appreciated his *Ideology* and his *Logic*. M. de Tracy was given his chair in the Academy by those affected little orators who saw him only as the author of a good grammar book and even then he was duly insulted by that pedestrian fellow Ségur, father of an even more pedestrian son, Philippe, who wrote about our misfortunes in Russia so as to earn a blue ribbon from Louis XVIII. That vile Philippe de Ségur will serve me as an example of the kind of character I most hate in Paris: the ministerial type of man faithful to honour in all things, except the actions that play a decisive part in one's life. Recently, this Philippe played towards the minister Casimir Perier (see the *Débats*, May 1832) the role that had earned him the favour of Napoleon whom he deserted in such a cowardly way, and then the favour of Louis XVIII who took a liking to this base kind of person. He understood their baseness perfectly well, and would recall it with a few well-chosen words when they were doing something noble. Perhaps the friend of Favras, who waited to hear whether he was going to be hanged before saying to one of his gentlemen in waiting, '*You can have dinner served now*,' had a touch of this character.[20] He was a man quite able to admit to himself that he was vile and to laugh at his vileness.

I sense, of course, that the term 'vile' is misapplied in this case, but this baseness, typical of Philippe Ségur and men like him, has always been my *bête noire*. I have a hundred times more esteem and affection for an ordinary convict, an ordinary murderer who yielded to a moment of weakness and who, moreover, was usually dying of starvation. In 1828 or [18]26, friend Philippe was busy giving a child to a million-airess, a widow he had seduced and who had to marry him (Mme Grefulhe, widow of a peer of the realm). I'd dined several times with this General Philippe de Ségur at the Emperor's service table. On those occasions, old Philippe only talked about his thirteen wounds, for he's a courageous brute.

He'd be a hero in Russia, in those half-civilised countries. In France, people are starting to see through his baseness. Mesdames Garnett (rue Duphot, No. 12) wanted to take me to the home of his brother, their neighbour, No. 14, I think, something I always refused because of the historian of the Russian Campaign.

The Count de Ségur, Grand Master of Ceremonies at Saint-Cloud in 1811, when I was there, was dying of chagrin that he wasn't a duke. In his view, this was worse than a misfortune, it was a *breach of good manners*. All his ideas were *petty*, but he had a great number of them, on every subject. He saw ill breeding in everyone and everywhere, but with what grace did he not express that feeling!

What I liked in this poor man was the passionate love his wife had for him. Moreover, when I talked to him, it seemed to me I was conversing with an inhabitant of Lilliput. I met M. de Ségur, Grand Master of Ceremonies from 1810 to 1814, at the homes of Napoleon's ministers. I have not seen him since the fall of that great man, of whom he was one of the indulgences and one of the misfortunes.

Even the Dangeaus[21] of the Emperor's Court, and there were many of them, for instance my friend Baron Martial Daru, even those men couldn't restrain their laughter at the ceremonial invented by the Count de Ségur for Napoleon's wedding to Marie Louise of Austria, and especially for their first official meeting. However infatuated Napoleon was with the new uniform he could wear as king, he couldn't keep up the pretence, he made fun of it with Duroc, who told me. I think nothing was actually performed of this labyrinth of trivial details. If I had my papers from Paris with me here, I'd add the programme to the present ramblings about my life. It's more than worth a glance, you think you're reading some practical joke.

I sigh in 1832, and say to myself, 'and yet that's the point to which petty Parisian vanity had brought down an Italian: Napoleon!'

Where was I?… Good God, how badly written this is!

The Count de Ségur was above all sublime in the Council of State. This Council was respectable; it wasn't, in 1810, an assembly of pedants, people like Cousin, Jacqueminot, or ***, and others even more obscure (1832).

With the exception of his most implacable enemies, Napoleon had brought together, in his Council of State, the fifty least stupid

Frenchmen. There were different departments. Sometimes the War Department (where I was apprenticed under the admirable Gouvion Saint-Cyr) had to do with the Department of the Interior that M. de Ségur sometimes presided over, I don't know how, I think it was during the absence or illness of the hearty Regnault (de Saint-Jean-d'Angély).

In difficult matters, for instance that of the levying of the guards of honour in Piedmont*, of which I was one of the junior rapporteurs, the elegant, the perfect M. de Ségur, unable to think what to say, would bring his chair forward; but he did so in an incredibly comic way, grasping it between his widespread thighs.

Having laughed at his impotence, I said to myself, 'But maybe I'm the one who's wrong? Here we have the famous ambassador to Catherine the Great, who stole the pen of the English ambassador.[22] He's the historian of William II or III (I've forgotten which, the lover of the Lichtenau woman over whom Benjamin Constant fought).'

I was too much inclined to *respect* people in my youth. When my imagination seized on a particular man, I would remain dumbstruck in his presence: *I adored his very failings*.

But the ridiculous idea of M. de Ségur guiding Napoleon was evidently too much for my *gullibility*[23].

Moreover, the Count de Ségur, Grand Master of Ceremonies (in this respect completely different from Philippe) could have been asked to show all his delicate touches, in the case of women rising to a degree of heroism. He also had delicate and charming turns of phrase, but they had to make sure not to rise above the Lilliputian littleness of his ideas.

I was really quite wrong not to cultivate the acquaintance of this amiable old man from 1821 to 1830; I think he passed away at the same time as his respectable wife. But I was crazy, my revulsion for everything vile was a real passion. Instead of being amused by it, as I am these days by the actions of the Court of *** The Count de Ségur had conveyed his compliments to me in 1817, on my return from England, on *Rome, Naples and Florence*, a little book I'd sent him.

In the depths of my heart**, from a moral point of view, I've always

* 23 June [1832].
** 23 June 1832.

despised Paris. To find popularity there, you had to be like M. de Ségur the Grand Master.

From a geographical point of view, I've never liked Paris. Even around 1803, I hated it because there were no mountains surrounding it. The mountains of my region (Dauphiné), witnesses of the passionate impulses of my heart during the first sixteen years of my life, gave me a *bias*[24] (a habit of mind: English term) on the subject, which I have never managed to get over.

I started to esteem Paris only on 28th July 1830[25]. Even on the day of the ordinances, at eleven o'clock in the evening, I was making fun of the bravery of the Parisians and the resistance they were being expected to show, at the home of Count Réal. I think that this eminently cheerful man and his heroic daughter, Baroness Lacuée, have still not forgiven me for it.

These days, I esteem Paris. I confess that, for courage, it has to be set in the foremost rank, as it does for cookery, and for *wit*. But I am still no more enamoured of it. It strikes me that there's always an element of *play-acting* in its virtue. Young men born in Paris from provincial fathers, endowed with masculine energy which has enabled them to make their fortunes, strike me as *enfeebled* beings, only attentive to the outward appearance of their clothes, the good taste of their *grey hats*, the elegant cut of their cravats, like MM. Féburier, Viollet-le-Duc, etc. I can't imagine a man without a certain *masculine energy*, constancy and depth in his ideas, etc. All things that are as rare in Paris as a coarse or even *harsh* tone.

But I must finish this chapter here. So as to try not to lie and not to hide my faults, I've imposed on myself the task of writing these memories down at a rate of twenty pages a sitting, like a letter. After my decease, they'll publish them from the original manuscript. In this way I will perhaps achieve *truthfulness*, but I will also have to beg the reader (perhaps born this morning in the house next door) to forgive me for these dreadful digressions.

CHAPTER [FIVE]

I realise in 1832* (in general, my philosophy is that of the day I'm writing on – I was far from these ideas in 1821), I see, then, that I was a *mezzo termine*[26] between the energetic coarseness of General Gross, Count Regnault de Saint-Jean-d'Angély, and the somewhat Lilliputian, somewhat narrow graces of the Count de Ségur, and M. Petit, the manager of the Hôtel de Bruxelles, etc.

It was only baseness which made me a stranger to the extremes I fall between. Merely for lack of savoir faire, for lack of industry, as M. D. (M. de l'écluze), of the *Débats*, told me in reference to my books and the Institute,[27] I missed out, on five or six occasions, on the highest political, financial or literary fortune. By chance, all this came knocking on my door in succession. A tender reverie in 1821 and a philosophical and melancholic reverie later on (all vanity apart, a melancholy exactly like that of M. Jacques in *As You Like It*) has become such a pleasure for me that, when a friend comes up to me in the street, I'd give a paolo for him not to speak to me. Merely the sight of someone I know puts me in a bad mood. When I see such a person in the distance, and have to get ready to greet him, it puts me in a bad mood fifty paces in advance. Conversely, I love meeting friends in the evening, in society, on Saturdays at M. Cuvier's, on Sundays at M. de Tracy's, on Tuesdays at Mme Ancelot's, on Wednesdays at Baron Gérard's, etc., etc.

A man blessed with a little tact can easily see that he is putting me into a bad mood by talking to me in the street. 'Here's a man who doesn't think enough of my merit,' says that man's vanity, quite wrongly.

Hence my happiness in strolling proudly through a foreign town, Lancaster, Torre del Greco, etc., where I have arrived just an hour ago and where I'm sure that nobody will know me. Over the past few years I've started to miss this happiness. If it weren't for seasickness I'd enjoy heading off to travel in America. Would you believe it? I'd love to wear a mask; I'd be delighted to change my name. *The Thousand and One Nights*, a book that I adore, fills more than a quarter of my thoughts. I often think of Angelica's ring[28]; my sovereign pleasure would be to change myself into a tall, blond German, and to stroll round Paris in that guise.

* 23 June 1832, Mero.

I've just flicked through my pages and see that I'd got as far as M. de Tracy. That old man, so dapper, always dressed in black, with an immense green eye-shade, standing in front of his mantelpiece now on one foot, now on another, had a way of speaking that was poles apart from his writings. His conversation consisted entirely of fine and elegant flashes of insight; he hated forceful expressions as much as swear-words, and he writes like a mayor from the countryside. The forceful simplicity that I believe I had at that time could hardly have met with his approval. I had huge black sideburns which Mme Doligny made me feel ashamed of only a year later. My face, that of an Italian butcher, seemed not exactly to meet with the approval of the old colonel from the reign of Louis XVI.

M. de Tracy, the son of a widow, was born around 1765 with an income of three hundred thousand francs. His town house was in the rue de Tracy, near the rue Saint-Martin. He played the part of a trades-man without realising it, like a host of rich men in 1780. M. de Tracy built his road and lost two or three hundred thousand francs and so on. So I really believe that these days this man, so likeable when, round 1790, he was the lover of Mme de Praslin, this profound reasoner, has changed his income of three hundred thousand livres into thirty at the very most.

His mother, a woman of rare good sense, was perfectly at home at Court; thus, at the age of twenty-two, her son was a colonel, and colonel of a regiment where he found among the captains a Tracy, his cousin, apparently as noble as he himself, and to whom it never occurred to be shocked at the idea of seeing this little dandy of twenty-two coming to command the regiment in which he was serving.

This dandy who, as Mme de Tracy later told me, had such admirable impulses, nonetheless concealed a basic common sense. This mother, a rare woman, on learning that there was a philosopher in Strasbourg (and, note well, this was in 1780, perhaps, not a philosopher like Voltaire, Diderot, Raynal), on learning, as I was saying, that there was in Strasbourg a philosopher who analysed the thoughts of man, the images or signs of all that he has seen, all that he has felt, realised that the science of turning over these images in his head would, if her son learnt it, make him a brainbox.

Just imagine what a brain must have been possessed in 1785 by a really handsome young man, from the high nobility, altogether at home at Court, with an income of three hundred thousand livres.

The Marquise de Tracy had her son placed in the artillery, which, two years running, took him to Strasbourg. If I ever go there, I'll ask who that German philosopher was, who was famous there around 1780.[29]

Two years later, I think, M. de Tracy was at Rethel, I think, with his regiment, which, I believe, was the Dragoons, something I can check in the *Royal Almanac* of the time.

The lemons*...

M. de Tracy never told me about those lemons; I found out the story from another misanthrope, a M. Jacquemont, an ex-monk, and, what's more, a man of the greatest merit. But M. de Tracy told me a great number of anecdotes about the first army of France as it reformed; M. de La Fayette was its commander in chief.

His l[ieutenan]t-colonel wanted to take the regiment off into emigration...

His leave and duel...

He was tall in stature, and, at the top of that big body, an imperturbable countenance, cold, as insignificant as an old family portrait, his head covered by a poorly made short wig. This man wearing some poorly made grey suit, hobbling somewhat and leaning on a walking stick as he entered the salon of Mme de Tracy who called him 'My dear Monsieur' in an enchanting tone of voice – such was General de La Fayette in 1821, and such he has been depicted by the Gascon painter Scheffer, in his portrait that is a very good likeness.

That *Dear Monsieur* of Mme de Tracy's, said in such a tone of voice, was, I believe, a cause of unhappiness to M. de Tracy. Not that M. de La Fayette was too friendly with his wife, or that he was bothered, at his age, by that kind of unhappiness; it's quite simply that the sincere admiration, never put on or exaggerated, shown by Mme de Tracy

* 23 June 1832, Mero.

32

for M. de La Fayette, established the latter too evidently as the main personage of the salon.

However much of an absolute beginner I was in 1821 (I'd always lived in the illusions of enthusiasm and of the passions) I managed to make this out *all by myself*.

I also sensed, without anyone telling me, that M. de La Fayette was quite simply a hero from Plutarch. He lived from day to day, without too much thought, quite simply performing, like Epaminondas[30], the great actions that presented themselves. And meanwhile, despite his age (born in 1757, like his companion in the tennis courts, Charles X), solely intent on squeezing from behind the skirts of some pretty girl (*vulgô*: feeling up her backside), frequently and without so much as a by-your-leave.

While waiting for great actions, which don't present themselves every day, and for the opportunity to squeeze the skirts of young women, which only ever really comes along at half-past midnight, as they are leaving, M. de La Fayette would explain rather inelegantly the commonplace philosophy of the National Guard. That government is good, and that government alone, which guarantees the citizen's security on the highways, his equality before the judges, and judges who are reasonably enlightened, as well as a coinage that is not debased, decent roads, and proper protection when abroad. Arranged in this manner, it's not too complicated a business.*

It has to be admitted that there's a huge difference between a man like that and M. de Ségur, the Grand Master; and France, Paris in particular, will be execrable in the eyes of posterity for not having recognised this great man.

For me, used to Napoleon and Lord Byron, and, let me add, to Lord Brougham, Monti, Canova, and Rossini,[31] I immediately recognised the grandeur of M. de La Fayette and I haven't changed my mind. I saw him on the July Days with his shirt full of holes; he treated with civility all the plotters, all the fools, all those who were strutting about giving themselves airs. He treated *me* less civilly; he asked that my old position be taken from me (and given to a coarse secretary, named Levasseur). Still, it never occurred to me to get cross or to venerate him any less, any

* 23 June [18]32, Mero.

more than it occurs to me to blaspheme against the sun when it is covered by a cloud.

M. de La Fayette, at that tender age of seventy-five, has the same failing as myself. He's passionate about a young Portuguese woman of eighteen, who's turned up in the salon of M. de Tracy, where she's the friend of his granddaughters, Mlles Georges La Fayette, de Lasteyrie, de Maubourg. He imagines, for this young Portuguese and for every other young woman, he imagines that she notices him, he dreams only of her, and the funny thing is he is often right to imagine all this. His European fame, the innate elegance of his speech, despite his apparent simplicity, his eyes that light up as soon as they find themselves a foot away from a pair of nice breasts, all this combines to help him pass his last years merrily, to the great scandal of women of thirty-five (the Marquise de Marmier (Choiseul), Mme de Perret and others) who come to this salon. None of those fine people can understand that it is possible to be amiable in any way other than the little witticisms of M. de Ségur or the sparkling reflections of M. Benjamin Constant.

M. de La Fayette is extremely polite and even affectionate towards everyone, but polite *like a king*. This is what I said one day to Mme de Tracy who got angry – insofar as grace incarnate can get angry – but perhaps from that day on she realised that the vigorous simplicity of my speech wasn't the same as the silliness of M. Dunoyer, for example. He was a good old liberal, today the moral prefect of Moulins, the best-intentioned, the most heroic perhaps and the silliest of the liberal writers... Take my word for it, since I'm on the same side as them, and that's saying a lot. The naive, open-mouthed admiration of M. Dunoyer, the editor of the *Censeur*, and that of two or three others of the same calibre, ceaselessly surrounded the general's armchair; as soon as he could, and to their great scandal, he would leave them standing, to go and admire from close up, with eyes aflame, the pretty shoulders of some young woman who had just come in. Those poor *virtuous* men (all of whom have sold themselves since, like ***, to the minister Perier, 1832) pulled comic faces at their abandonment and I made fun of them, which scandalised my new lady friend. But it was understood that she had a thing for me. 'There's a *spark in him*,' she said one day to a lady, one of those ladies tailor-made to admire the Lilliputian witticisms of

Ségur's type, who was complaining to her of the severe and frank simplicity with which I was telling her that all those ultraliberals were doubtless perfectly respectable through their high-minded virtue, but in other respects incapable of understanding that two and two make four.[32] The clumsiness, slowness, and virtue that, taking alarm at the least truth told to the Americans – all these things on the part of a Dunoyer, a ***, or a ***, is really beyond belief; it's like the absence of any but commonplace ideas in a Ludovic Vitet, a Mortimer Ternaux, the new generation that renewed the Tracy salon around 1828. In the midst of all this, M. de La Fayette was and is without doubt still a *Party Leader*.

He must have picked up this habit in 1789. The essential thing is not to offend anyone and to remember everyone's name, and he's admirably good at that. The active and urgent interest of a party leader keeps M. de La Fayette away from any *literary ideas*, and in any case I think he's quite incapable of any. It is, I think, by this mechanism that he didn't feel how very clumsy and boring the writings of M. Dunoyer and consorts were.

I was forgetting to depict this salon. Sir Walter Scott and his imitators would have docilely begun with those details*, but I hate material description. The tedium of having to do it stops me writing novels.

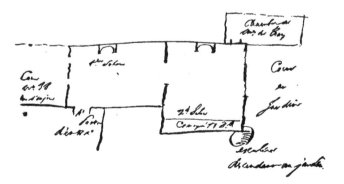

* 23rd June 1832, third day's work. Did between 60 and 90.

The main door A admits you into a long salon, at the end of which there is a big double door always open. You come to quite a big square salon with a fine lamp in the shape of a chandelier and on the mantel-piece a horrid little clock*. On the right as you go into this big salon, there is a fine blue divan on which are sitting fifteen girls aged between twelve and eighteen and their suitors: M. Charles de Rémusat, who has a great deal of wit and even more affectation. He's a copy of the famous actor Fleury. M. François de Corcelles who has all the frank and rough manners of a Republican. He probably sold himself in 1831; in 1820, he already published a small book that had the misfortune to be praised by the solicitor M. Dupin (a patent villain, and known as such by me as early as 1827). In 1821, MM. de Rémusat and de Corcelles were men of some distinction and have since married granddaughters of M. de La Fayette. At their side appeared a cold Gascon, M. Scheffer, a painter. He is, it seems to me, the most shameless liar and has the most ignoble face I know. I was assured that in bygone days he paid court to the celestial ***, the oldest of M. de La Fayette's granddaughters, who has since married the elder son of M. Augustin Perier, the most important and the most starchy of my compatriots. Mlle Virginie, I think, was the favourite lady friend of Mme de Tracy.

Next to the elegant M. de Rémusat could be seen two Jesuit faces with their insincere, sidelong glances. The two of them were brothers and they had the privilege of talking for hours at a time to the Count de Tracy. I adored then with all the vivacity of youth, in 1821 (I was barely twenty-one years old when it came to the heart's gullibility). Having soon seen through them, my enthusiasm for M. de Tracy suffered a noticeable decrease.

The elder of these brothers has published a sentimentalising history of William's conquest of England. He's M. Thierry from the Academy of Inscriptions.[33] He has had the merit of restoring their authentic spelling to Clovis, Chilpéric, Thierry et al., all the phantoms of the earliest periods of our history. He has published a less sentimental volume on the organisation of the communes in France in 1200. A schoolboy vice has made him blind. His brother, much more of a Jesuit (in his heart and his behaviour) although an ultraliberal like the other,

* 23rd June.

became prefect of Vesoul in 1830 and probably sold himself for the sake of his salary, like his patron, M. Guizot.

In perfect contrast to these two Jesuit brothers, to the clumsy Dunoyer, to the dandyish Rémusat, was the young Victor Jacquemont, who has since travelled in India. Victor was really lean then; he is more than six foot tall, and in those days he didn't have the least sense of logic, and in consequence, he was a misanthrope. On the pretext that he was a man of great wit, M. Jacquemont didn't want to take the trouble to reason. This true Frenchman regarded an invitation to reason as a literal piece of insolence. Travel was really the only door that vanity left open to the truth. Besides, I may be wrong. Victor strikes me as a man of the greatest distinction; I am like a connoisseur (if you'll pardon the expression) who can see a fine horse in a four-month foal whose legs are still swollen. He became my friend, and this morning (1832) I received a letter he wrote me from Kashmir, in India.

His heart had just a single failing: a low and parochial envy of Napoleon. This envy was moreover the sole passion I have ever seen in the Count de Tracy. It was with indescribable pleasure that the old metaphysician and big Victor would relate the anecdote of the rabbit-hunt to which M. de Talleyrand invited Napoleon, who at the time had been First Consul for six weeks, and was already thinking of mimicking Louis XIV.

The rabbits in the barrel and the pigs in the Bois de Boulogne.

Victor had the failing of being very much in love with Mme Lavenelle, the wife of a spy with an income of forty thousand [francs] and entrusted with the task of reporting back to the Tuileries the actions and the remarks of G[ener]al La Fayette. The funny thing is that the general, Benjamin Constant, and M. Bignon took this M. de Lavenelle into their confidence when coming out with all their liberal ideas. As can be guessed in advance, this spy, a terrorist in '93, only ever talked of marching to the château to massacre all the Bourbons. His wife was such a libertine, so much in love with the physical man, that she finally put me right off all *loose* talk in French. I love that kind of conversation in Italian; ever since my earliest youth, as a sub-lieutenant in the 6th Dragoons, I was horrified to hear it in the mouth* of Mme Henriett, the Captain's

* 23 Ju[ne].

37

wife. This Mme Lavenelle is as dry as a piece of parchment and in any case has no wit, and above all no *passion*, and it's quite impossible for her to be affected other than by the sturdy thighs of a company of grenadiers parading through the garden of the Tuileries in white kerseymere knickerbockers.

The same could not be said of Mme Baraguey d'Hilliers of that ilk, whom I soon got to know at the home of Mme Beugnot. Nor could it be said of Mme Ruga and Mme Aresi, in Milan. In a word, I hate licentious remarks in French; the mixture of wit and emotion jars upon my soul, just as the sound of cork being cut with a knife offends my ear.

The moral description of this salon is perhaps rather long; there are only two or three more figures to mention.

The charming Louise Letort, daughter of G[ener]al Letort, of the Dragoons of the Guard, whom I knew very well in Vienna in 1809. Mlle Louise, who turned into such a beauty and who, up until now, has had so little affectation in her character and at the same time so much elevation, was born the day before or the day after Waterloo. Her mother, the charming Sarah Newton, married M. Victor de Tracy, the son of the peer of the realm, then an infantry major.

We called him Rod of Iron. That was the definition of his character. Brave, wounded several times in Spain under Napoleon, he has the misfortune of seeing the bad side of everything. A week ago (June 1832), King Louis-Philippe dissolved the artillery regiment of the National Guard, of which M. Victor de Tracy was colonel. As a *député*, he speaks frequently and has the misfortune of being too polite when it is his turn to speak. You'd think he daren't speak his mind. Like his father, he was pettily jealous of Napoleon. Now that the hero is dead and gone, he is more in evidence, but the hero was still alive when I started out in the salon of the rue d'Anjou. I saw the joy that his death occasioned there. Everyone's eyes expressed the thought: we'd always said that a bourgeois who became a king could never come to a good end.

I lived for ten years in this salon, received politely, well esteemed, but every day less *close* to people, except to my friends. That's one of the failings of my character. It's this failing which means that I don't blame men for my lack of advancement. That, it must be said, despite what G[ener]al Duroc told me on two or three occasions of my talents for the military – I'm happy to stay in an inferior position. Admirably content, above all, when I'm two hundred leagues away from my boss, like today.

So I hope that, if boredom doesn't stop people reading this book, they won't find any sense of grievance against men. You only fish for their favours. When I wish to use them, I fish out a mark of esteem or two, but soon my hand wearies of having to dangle the hook. And yet, in 1814, when Napoleon sent me to join the Seventh Division, Countess Daru, a minister's wife, said to me, 'If it weren't for this damned invasion, you'd have been appointed prefect of an important city.' I had some reason to believe it was Toulouse.

I was forgetting an odd character, a woman; I neglected to please her, she turned into an enemy of mine. Mme de Montcertin, tall and well proportioned, very shy, lazy, completely in thrall to force of habit, had two lovers: one for the town, the other for the country, each of them as unlovely as the other. This arrangement lasted for I don't know how many years. I think it was the painter Scheffer who was the lover in the country; the lover in the town was Colonel, today G[ener]al Carbonel, who had had himself appointed General La Fayette's bodyguard.

One day the eight or ten nieces of Mme de Montcertin asked her what love was; she replied, 'It's a nasty thing which chambermaids are sometimes accused of, and when they are found guilty of it, they are dismissed.'

I should have played the gallant with Mme Montcertin. There was no danger in it; I'd never have succeeded, for she was happy to stick with her two men and was terribly afraid of getting pregnant. But I viewed her as a *thing* and not as a human being. She took her revenge by repeating three or four times a week that I was a superficial, half-mad person. She would make tea, and it's all too true that very often all evening long I would speak to her only at the moment she offered me some tea.

The number of people who had to be asked for their news when one entered this salon altogether put me off.

Apart from the fifteen or twenty granddaughters of M. de La Fayette or their girl friends, almost all of them blond with shining complexions and rather ordinary faces (it's true that I was just back from Italy) who were sitting drawn up in battle formation on the divan, you had to say hello to:

Countess de Tracy – sixty-three years old;

Count de Tracy – sixty years;

General La Fayette;

His son George Washington La Fayette (a true citizen of the United States of America, perfectly free of any ideas of nobility);

Mme de Tracy, my friend, had a son;

M. Victor de Tracy, born round 1785,

Mme Sarah de Tracy, his wife, young and brilliant, a model of delicate English beauty, a bit too skinny,

and two daughters, Mesdames Georges de La Fayette and de l'Aubépin.

You also had to greet the great M. de l'Aubépin, the author, with a monk he kept and fed, of the *Memorial*. Always there, he said eight or ten words per evening.

For a long time I thought Mme Georges de La Fayette was a nun whom Mme de Tracy had brought to live in her home out of charity. With this turn of mind, she has ideas as sharp and fixed as if she were a Jansenist. But she had four or five daughters at least. Mme de Maubourg, M. de La Fayette's daughter, had five or six. It took me ten years to distinguish between all these blond faces saying things that were *perfectly respectable* but enough to send me to sleep, accustomed as I was to the eloquent eyes and the bold character of the beautiful women of Milan, and before that to the adorable simplicity of those fine women of Germany. (I was on the Quartermaster-General's staff in Sagan, Silesia, and Brunswick.)

M. de Tracy had been the close friend of the celebrated Cabanis[34], the father of materialism, whose book (*Relations Between the Physical and the Moral*) had been my bible at the age of sixteen. Mme Cabanis and her daughter, six foot tall and in spite of that very likeable, would appear in this salon. M. de Tracy took me to see them in their home, in the rue des Vieilles-Tuileries, at the back of beyond; I was driven away by the heat. In those days, I had an entirely *Italian* nervous susceptibility. A closed room that had ten persons sitting in it was enough to make me feel dreadfully ill, and almost enough to make me fall in a faint. Just imagine a room completely closed and with a blazing fire.

I didn't spell out this physical weakness in enough detail; the fire drove me away from Mme Cabanis' home. M. de Tracy never forgave me. I could have said a word or two to Countess de Tracy, but in those days I was *as gauche as they come*, and still am, to some extent.

Mlle Cabanis, in spite of her height of six foot, wanted to get married; she married a little dancer with a well-groomed wig, M. Dupaty, a so-called sculptor, the author of the statue of Louis XIII on the Place Royale sitting astride a kind of mule. This mule is an Arab horse that I often saw at M. Dupaty's. This poor horse would be kicking its heels in a corner of the studio. M. Dupaty gave me a resounding welcome as a writer on Italy and the author of a history of painting. It was difficult to be more *respectable* and more devoid of warmth, spontaneity, impulsiveness, etc., than this fine fellow. The lowest of trades for those Parisians, so well groomed, so prim and proper, so *respectable*, is sculpture.

M. Dupaty, so polite, was moreover very brave, he should have stayed a soldier.

At Mme Cabanis', I got to know a very decent man, though very bourgeois, very narrow-minded, very meticulous in his whole petty household politics. The sole aim of M. Thurot, a professor of Greek, was to be a member of the Academy of Inscriptions. Through a dreadful paradox, this man, who never blew his nose without thinking of maintaining his vanity in such a way as to influence from a distance of a thousand leagues his nomination to the Academy, was an *ultraliberal*. This brought us together at first, but soon his wife, a bourgeois woman to whom I never spoke except under duress, found me imprudent.

One day, M. de Tracy and M. Thurot asked me for my political opinions, I alienated both of them with my reply:

'As soon as I came to power, I would republish the list of émigrés, declaring that Napoleon usurped a power that did not belong to him when he struck their names out. Three quarters of them are dead; I'd exile the rest to the *départements* of the Pyrénées and two or three nearby. I'd have these four or five *départements* surrounded by two or three small armies which, to create the right moral impact, would bivouac there at least six months of the year. Any émigré who left would be shot without mercy.

41

'Their possessions returned by Napoleon, sold piecemeal, not exceeding two acres, the émigrés would enjoy fixed incomes of one thousand, two thousand, three thousand francs per annum. They would be able to choose somewhere to live in a foreign country. But if they went round stirring up intrigue, no more pardon.'

The faces of MM. Thurot and de Tracy fell more and more as I explained this plan; I seemed atrocious to those petty souls enfeebled by the politeness of Paris. A young woman who was present admired my ideas, and especially the excessive imprudence with which I laid them bare, she saw in me the *Huron* (of Voltaire's novel).[35]

This young woman's extreme benevolence consoled me for many of my failures. I was never entirely her lover. She was extremely coquettish, extremely obsessed with jewellery, always talking about handsome men, closely acquainted with all the most brilliant people in the boxes at the Opera Buffa.

I'm changing the details a bit so she won't be recognised. If I'd been sensible enough to intimate to her that I loved her, she'd probably have been delighted. The fact is that I didn't love her enough to forget that I'm not handsome. She herself had forgotten the fact. On one of the occasions when I was leaving Paris, she said to me in the middle of my salon, 'I've got something to tell you,' and, in a passage that led to an antechamber which was fortunately empty, she gave me a kiss on the lips, and I returned it with ardour. I left the next day and everything finished there.

But, before we got to this point, we *spoke to each other* for several years, as people say in Champagne. She would faithfully relate to me, whenever I asked, all the bad things people were saying about me.

She had a charming tone, she seemed neither to approve nor to disapprove. To have a Minister of Police here is what I find most welcome in love affairs which are, it has to be said, so frigid in Paris.

People have no idea of the atrocious things that you can learn. One day she said to me, 'M***, the spy, said at M. de Tracy's: "Oh look! It's M. Beyle with a new suit; evidently, Mme Pasta has just had a benefit."'

This stupid remark gave great pleasure. M. de Tracy couldn't forgive me for this liaison (as public as it was innocent) with the celebrated actress.

What adds salt to the anecdote is the fact that Céline, who was reporting the spy's words to me, was perhaps herself jealous of my assiduity at the home of Mme Pasta.

No matter what time my evenings out finished elsewhere, I would go to Mme Pasta's (rue de Richelieu, opposite the National Library, Hôtel des Lillois, No. 63). I was staying a hundred yards or so away, at No. 47. Fed up with the angry porter who was so vexed at often having to open up to me at three in the morning, I ended up staying in the same house as Mme Pasta. A fortnight later I found my credit had dropped seventy per cent in Mme de Tracy's salon. I made the greatest mistake in not consulting my friend Mme de Tracy. My behaviour at that time was nothing but a series of caprices. If I'd been a marquis, or a colonel, with an income of forty thousand francs, I'd have managed to destroy myself.

I passionately loved, not music as such, but simply the music of Cimarosa and Mozart.[36] The salon of Mme Pasta was the meeting-place for all the Milanese who came to Paris. Because of them, sometimes, by chance, I heard mention of the name of Métilde.

Métilde in Milan learnt that I was spending all my time with an actress. This idea perhaps finally cured her.

I was perfectly blind to all that. For an entire summer, I played faro[37] until daybreak at Mme Pasta's, silent, delighted to hear Milanese being spoken, and breathing in the idea of Métilde through every sense. I would go up into my charming room on the third floor, and correct, with tears in my eyes, the proofs of *On Love*. This is a book I sketched out in Milan, in my lucid intervals. Working on it in Paris made me feel ill, I never wanted to tidy it up.

Men of letters say, 'In all foreign countries, people may have ingenious thoughts, but they know how to *write a book* only in France.' Yes, if the sole aim of a book is to *get an idea across to the reader*, no, if the author hopes at the same time to make the reader feel, to communicate some nuance of emotion.

The French rule is only valid for a work of history, for example the *History of the Regency*, by M. Lemontey, whose authentically academic style I was admiring this morning. The preface of M. Lemontey (a miser whom I got to well know at Count Beugnot's) can be taken as a model of that academic style.

I'd certainly please the foolish if I took the trouble to organise like that some of the passages of the present ramblings. But perhaps, writing this like a letter, thirty pages a sitting, I can make it seem *real without knowing*.

For, more than anything else, I want to be truthful. What a miracle it would be in this century of play-acting, in a society in which three quarters of the actors are such bare-faced charlatans as M. Magendie or Count Regnault de Saint-Jean-d'Angély, or Baron Gérard!

One of the characteristics of the Revolutionary generation (1789–1832) is that there is no success without a certain degree of shamelessness and even of out-and-out charlatanism. M. de La Fayette alone is above charlatanism which must here be distinguished from a warm and welcoming manner, the *necessary weapon* of a party leader.

I'd got to know at Mme Cabanis' a man who, to be sure, is no charlatan, M. Fauriel (Mme Condorcet's ex-lover). He is, with M. Mérimée and myself, the only example known to myself of non-charlatanism when it comes to those involved in the trade of writing.

M. Fauriel thus has no reputation. One day, the bookseller Bossanges conveyed an offer to me: I'd get fifty copies of one of his works if I was prepared not just to write a nice article publicising it, but to get it published in some newspaper or other where I was at the time (for a fortnight) in favour. I was scandalised and said that I'd write the article for just one copy. Soon, disgust at having to court dirty cads like that led me to stop seeing those journalists and I have to say it weighs on my conscience that I never wrote the article.

But this happened in 1826 or 1827. Let's go back to 1821. M. Fauriel, treated with contempt by Mme Condorcet on his death (she was a woman who only valued physical pleasure), often went to see a little half-humpbacked shrew, Mlle Clarke.

She was an Englishwoman who was undeniably witty, but her wit was like the horns of a chamois: dry, hard and twisted. M. Fauriel, who in those days prized my merits highly, soon took me to Mlle Clarke's; there I bumped into my old friend Augustin Thierry (the author of the history of William and the Conquest) who ruled the roost there. I was struck by the superb face of Mme Belloc (the wife of the painter) who bore an astonishing resemblance to Lord Byron whom I greatly liked at the time. A perceptive man who considered me to be a real Machiavelli, because I'd just got back from Italy, said to me, 'Can't you see you'll waste your time with Mme Belloc? She makes love with Mlle Montgolfier (a horrid little monster with lovely eyes).'

I was thunderstruck, both at my Machiavellianism, and at my alleged love for Mme Belloc, and even more at this lady's love. Perhaps there's something in the story.

After a year or two, Mlle Clarke picked a quarrel over nothing with me, after which I stopped seeing her, and M. Fauriel, to my intense annoyance, followed suit. MM. Fauriel and Victor Jacquemont rise to an immense height above all my acquaintances in these first months of my return to Paris. Countess de Tracy was at least on the same high level. In fact, I surprised or scandalised* all my acquaintances. I was a Monster or a God. Even today, the whole of Mlle Clarke's circle firmly believes that I'm a monster:

A monster of immorality above all. The reader knows the facts of the matter, that I'd consorted with whores only once, and perhaps will remember my successes with that celestially beautiful girl, Alexandrine.

This is what my life was like at that period. I got up at ten o'clock and at half-past ten I was at the Café de Rouen, where I met Baron de Lussinge and my cousin Colomb (a man of integrity and justice, reasonable, my childhood friend). The problem is that these two people understood absolutely nothing** of the theory of the human heart or the depiction of this heart in literature and music. Reflecting on this subject far and wide, and dwelling on the consequences to be drawn from each new *and properly proven* anecdote, constitute far and away the most interesting conversation for me. Subsequently it turned out that M. Mérimée, whom I so greatly esteem, didn't enjoy this kind of conversation either. My childhood friend, the excellent Crozet (Chief Engineer of the département of the Isère), excels in the genre. But his wife has stolen him away from me for a number of years, jealous of our friendship. What a shame! What a superior man this M. Crozet would have been if he'd lived in Paris! Marriage and especially life in the

* Saturday, 23rd June.
** 1832, Saturday 23rd, Midsummer's Eve. *Made*[38] 30 pages. 24th June [18]32, Midsummer's Day.

45

provinces age a m[an] to an astonishing extent: the mind grows lazy, and any effort on the part of the brain becomes more and more rare and thus laborious and before long impossible.

Having enjoyed in the Café de Rouen our excellent cup of coffee and two brioches, I would accompany Lussinge to his office. We'd go through the Tuileries and along the Seine embankments, stopping off at every stall selling engravings. When I left Lussinge the most dismal time of the day would begin for me. I went, in that year's great heat, to seek the shade and a little coolness beneath the great chestnut trees of the Tuileries. 'Since I can't forget her, wouldn't I do better to kill myself?' I'd think. Everything was burdensome to me. I still had in 1821 that residual passion for painting in Italy which had made me write on that subject in 1816 and '17. I'd go to the Museum with a ticket that Lussinge had procured for me. The sight of those masterpieces merely reminded me all the more intensely of Brera and Métilde. When I came across the corresponding French name in a book, I would change colour.

I have very few memories of those days, which were all the same. Everything that people like in Paris filled me with intense distaste. Although a liberal myself, I found the liberals outrageously inane. In short, I see that I've kept a memory that is sad and hurtful for me of all that I saw then.

Fat Louis XVIII, with his ox's eyes, slowly hauled everywhere by his six big horses, I met everywhere, and he filled me with particular distaste. I bought a few plays by Shakespeare, an English edition, at thirty sous each; I'd read them in the Tuileries and I'd often let the book fall so as to daydream about Métilde. The interior of my solitary room was terrible for me.

Finally, five o'clock came round; I'd rush over to the table d'hôte of the Hôtel de Bruxelles. There I'd meet Lussinge, gloomy, tired, bored, together with old friend Barot, the elegant Poitevin, five or six eccentrics of the kind that flock to tables d'hôte, a species that borders on the swindler on one side and on the subaltern conspirator on the other. At this table d'hôte I recognised M. Alpy, formerly General Michaud's aide-de-camp, who would go and fetch his boots for him. To my astonishment, seeing him here I found he'd become a colonel and the son-in-law of M. Kentzinger, rich, stupid, ministerial and Mayor of

Strasbourg. I never spoke to this colonel nor to his father-in-law. A lean man, quite tall, sallow and talkative caught my attention. There was something of the sacred flame of Jean-Jacques Rousseau in his phrases in favour of the Bourbons, which the whole table found superficial and ridiculous. This man had the bearing – poles apart from grace – of an Austrian officer; later on he became famous: he was M. Courvoisier, the Garde des Sceaux[39]. Lussinge had known him in Besançon.

After dinner, coffee was still a pleasant time for me. Quite the opposite of the stroll along the boulevard de Gand that was all the fashion and filled with dust. To be there, in that meeting-place of elegant subalterns, officers of the Guard, first-class whores and the elegant middle-class women who were their rivals, was real torment for me.[*]

There, I encountered one of my childhood friends, Count de Barral, a fine and excellent lad who was the grandson of a famous miser and was beginning at the age of thirty to feel the first incursions of that unhappy passion. The Marquis de Barral his grandfather…

Soup […];

gift father Dom[inique][40].

In 1810, I think it was, M. de Barral having lost all he had at gambling, I lent him a little money and forced him to leave for Naples. His father, a perfect gentleman, gave him an income of six thousand francs.

A few years later, Barral, back from Naples, found me living with an actress-singer who, every evening, at half-past eleven, would come and settle down in my bed. I would come home at one o'clock, and we'd have supper: a cold partridge and some champagne. This relationship lasted two or three years. Mlle B[éreyter] had a girlfriend, the daughter of the celebrated M. Rose, the seller of leather trousers. Molé, the famous actor, had seduced the three sisters, all charming girls. One of them is today the Marquise de D***. Anette, going from failure to failure, was living with a man who worked at the Stock Exchange. I sang her praises so much to Barral that he fell in love with her. I persuaded pretty Anette to leave her horrid speculator. Barral hardly had five francs coming in on the 2nd of each month. On the 1st,

[*] 24 June [1832].

47

returning from his banker's with five hundred francs, he would go to redeem his watch that he had pawned, and gamble the four hundred francs remaining to him. I made a real effort and gave two dinners to the belligerent parties, at Véry's, at the Tuileries, and I finally persuaded Anette to become the Count's housekeeper and to live sensibly [?] with him on the five hundred francs his father gave him. Today (1832), this domestic arrangement has lasted for ten years. Unfortunately, Barral has become rich: he has an income of twenty thousand francs at least, and with wealth he has become abominably miserly.

In 1817, I'd been very much in love with Anette for a fortnight; after this, I'd found her ideas *narrow and Parisian*. For me, this is the most effective remedy to love. In the evening, amid the dust of the boulevard de Gand, I'd meet up with this childhood friend and dear Anette. I didn't know what to say to them. I was perishing of boredom and sadness; the whores didn't cheer me up at all. Finally, around half-past ten I would go to Mme Pasta for a game of faro, and I had the discomfiture of being the first there and being reduced to the conversation, only fit for the kitchen, of old *Rachele*, mother of Giuditta. But she spoke to me in Milanese; sometimes I'd find with her some halfwit just back from Milan, whom she'd invited to dinner. I timidly asked this halfwit for news of all the pretty women in Milan. I would have died rather than mention Métilde's name, but sometimes they would spontaneously tell me about her. These evenings constituted an important episode in my life. Finally the game of faro would begin. Thereupon, absorbed in a profound reverie, I would lose or win thirty francs in four hours.

I'd so abandoned all concern with my honour that, when I lost more than I had in my pockets, I would say to the man who had won, 'Would you like me to go upstairs and get the money?' He would reply, '*No, si figuri!*'[41] And I would pay only the next day. This frequently repeated tactlessness gave me the reputation of a poor man. I realised as much later on from the lamentations uttered by the excellent Pasta, Judith's husband, when he saw me losing thirty or thirty-five francs. Even when I had been made aware of this detail, I didn't change my behaviour.

CHAPTER SIX

Sometimes I would write a date on a book that I bought and an indication of the feelings that were uppermost in me. Perhaps I'll find some date in my books. I really don't know how the idea of going to England occurred to me. I wrote to M***, my banker, asking him to give me a note of credit for a thousand écus to be drawn in London, he replied that he only had one hundred and twenty-six francs of mine. I had some money I don't know where, in Grenoble perhaps, I had it sent to me and I left.

My first idea of London came to me in this way in 1821. One day, around 1816, I think, in Milan, I was talking of suicide with the famous Brougham (today Lord Brougham, Chancellor, who will soon be dead of overwork).

'What could be more disagreeable,' said Brougham to me, 'than the idea that all the newspapers will announce that you've blown your brains out, and then rake over your private life to find out why you did it?… It's enough to put you off killing yourself.' – 'What could be simpler,' I replied, 'than* to pick up the habit of going on a sea trip with the fishing boats? One stormy day, you accidentally fall in.'

This idea of going on a sea trip seduced me. The only readable writer for me was Shakespeare, I really loved the idea of seeing him performed. I hadn't seen any Shakespeare in 1817, at the time of my first trip to England.

The only things I have passionately loved in my life are:

Cimarosa,

Mozart

and Shakespeare.

In Milan, in 1820, I wanted to put these words on my gravestone. Every day I would think of this inscription, firmly believing that I would have no peace of mind except in the grave. I wanted a marble slab in the shape of a playing-card.

* 24 June [1832].

Errico Beyle

Milanese

visse, scrisse, amò.

Quest'anima

adorava

Cimarosa, Mozart e Shakespeare

morì di anni ....

il . 18..

No filthy little sign to be added, no insipid ornament, this inscription[42] to be engraved in capital letters. I hate Grenoble, I arrived in Milan in May 1800, I love that city. There I found the greatest pleasures and the greatest pains, there above all what constitutes one's first homeland[:] I found my first pleasures. There I wish to spend my old age, and die.

How many times, on a solitary small boat rocked by the waves of Lake Como, did I say myself in delight:

Hic captabis frigus opacum.[43]

If I leave behind enough money for this slab to be made, I request that it be placed in the Andilly cemetery, near Montmorency, facing the east. But above all I wish to have no other monument, nothing Parisian, nothing smacking of vaudeville; I loathe that kind of thing. I loathed it even more in 1821. The French wit I encountered in the theatres of Paris almost made me shout out aloud, 'Riff-raff! Riff-raff! Riff-raff!' I would leave after the first act. When French music was joined to French wit, my *repugnance* was so great that it almost made me start to pull faces and make a spectacle of myself. Mme Longueville gave me, one day, her box in the Feydeau Theatre. Fortunately, I didn't take anyone else with me. I fled after a quarter of an hour, pulling ridiculous faces and swearing that I wouldn't set foot in the Feydeau for two years: I kept this vow.

Everything that resembles the novels of Mme de Genlis, the poetry of MM. Legouvé, Jouy, Campenon, Treneuil, filled me with the same repugnance. There's nothing more commonplace than writing this in 1832, everyone else thinks the same. In 1821, Lussinge made fun of my intolerable pride whenever I made a show of my convulsive hatred. He drew the conclusion that M. de Jouy or M. Campenon had doubtless written a savage criticism of some of my works. A critic who has made fun of me fills me with quite different feelings. I think over his criticism each time I reread it, and try to decide who is right, him or me.

It was, it seems to me, in September 1821 that I left for London. I felt only disgust for Paris. I was blind, I should have asked for advice from the Countess de Tracy. This adorable woman and loved by me as a mother – no, as an ex-pretty woman, but without any idea of earthly love – was at the time sixty-three years old. I had rejected her friendship through my lack of confidence. I should have been the friend, no, the lover of Céline. I don't know if I would have succeeded as a lover at the time, but I can clearly see today that I was on the verge of an intimate friendship. I should never have rejected the opportunity to renew my acquaintance with Countess Berthois.

I was in despair, or, more precisely, profoundly wearied with life in Paris, and above all with myself. I detected every failing in myself; I would have liked to be someone else. I went off to London to find a remedy for the spleen and I more or less found it. I had to place a hill between myself and the sight of the *Duomo* of Milan. The plays of Shakespeare and the actor Kean[44] were this event. As often as not I would encounter in society people who would come up and compliment me on one of my works; I'd written very few at the time. And once the compliment had been paid and replied to, we didn't know what else to say to each other. Those Parisian flatterers, expecting some vaudeville reply, must have found me really gauche and perhaps really haughty. I am used to appearing the opposite of what I really am. I regard and have always regarded my works as lottery tickets. The only thing I esteem is the idea of being reprinted in 1900. Petrarch counted on his Latin poem *Africa* and hardly spared a thought for his sonnets.

Among the flatterers, there were two who paid me particular compliments. The one, fifty years old, a tall and strikingly handsome man, bore an astonishing likeness to *Jupiter Mansuetus*[45]. In 1821, I was still filled with the wild joy that had led me to write, four years previously, the beginning of the second volume of the *History of Painting*. This very handsome flatterer spoke with the same affectedness you find in Voltaire's letters; he had been condemned to death in Naples in 1800 or 1799. His name was *di Fiori* and today he happens to be the dearest of my friends. We went for ten years without understanding each other; in those days I didn't know how to respond to his quibbles à la Voltaire.

The second flatterer had superb blond English hair, nice and curly. He must have been about thirty and his name was *Edward Edwards*. A former ne'er-do-well from the streets of London and a war commissioner, I think, in the army of occupation commanded by the Duke of Wellington. Subsequently, when I learnt that he'd been a ne'er-do-well on the streets of London, working for the papers, trying to dream up a play on words that would become famous, I was quite astonished that he wasn't some swindler. Poor Edward Edwards had another quality: he was naturally and perfectly brave. So naturally that he, who boasted about everything with a more than French vanity, if such a thing is possible, and without French restraint, never mentioned his bravery.

I met M. Edward in the coach to Calais. Finding himself with a French author, he felt obliged to talk and this cheered me up no end. I'd been counting on the landscape to keep me interested. There's nothing so flat and monotonous (for me at least) as the road through Abbeville, Montreuil-sur-Mer, etc. Those long white roads stretching into the distance across a slightly undulating terrain would have made me feel quite gloomy without the chatter of Edwards.

However, the walls of Montreuil and the stoneware used to serve lunch in reminded me vividly of England.

We were travelling with a certain *Schmit*, the ex-secretary of the most pettily scheming of men, the Councillor of State Fréville, whom I'd got to know at the home of Mme Nardot, rue de Menars, No. 4. This poor Schmidt, at first a decent enough man, had ended up becoming a political spy. M. Decazes would send him to the congresses at the spa town of Aix-la-Chapelle. Still scheming and eventually, I think, stealing, changing fortune every six months, one day *Schmidt* met me and told me that, as a marriage *of convenience* and not of inclination, he was going to marry the daughter of Marshal Oudinot, the Duke of Reggio, who, in point of fact, has a whole regiment of daughters, and would ask Louis XVIII for alms every six months.

'Marry this evening, my dear friend,' I told him in surprise. But I learnt, a fortnight later, that Duke Decazes, unfortunately learning of the fortune of this poor Schmidt, had felt obliged to write a note to the father-in-law. But Schmidt was not such a bad fellow, and quite a decent companion.

At Calais, I made a silly mistake. I talked at the table d'hôte like a man who hasn't talked for a year. I was very cheerful. I almost got drunk on English beer. A half-yokel, the English skipper of an inshore vessel, made a few objections to my stories, I replied to him cheerfully and good-naturedly. That night I had a terrible attack of indigestion, for the first time in my life. Some days later *Edwards* told me in measured tones, something exceedingly rare for him, that in Calais I should have replied sharply and not cheerfully to the English captain.

This dreadful mistake is one I committed on one other occasion in 1813, in Dresden, towards M***, who has since lost his mind. I am not lacking in bravery, such a thing wouldn't happen to me again these days. But in my youth when I used to improvise, I was quite wild. My whole attention was focused on the beauty of the images I was trying to express. M. Edwards' warning was for me what the cock crow was for St Peter. For two days we looked for the English captain in all the filthy taverns that those sort of people frequent near the tower, I think.

On the second day, I believe, Edwards told me in measured tones, politely and even elegantly, 'Every nation, you see, has a certain particular way of fighting; our English manner is baroque, etc., etc., etc.' Anyway, the result of all this philosophy was that he requested me to let him speak to the captain who, ten to one, despite the national antipathy towards the French, would say that he had not had the slightest intention to offend me, etc., etc., etc. But anyway, if it should come to a duel, Edwards begged me to allow him to fight in my place.

'Are you trying to make a bloody fool of me?' I said to him. There were harsh words between us, but finally he convinced me that for his part there was nothing but an excess of zeal and we set off in search of the captain once more. Two or three times I felt all the hair on my arms rise, thinking that I'd recognised the captain. I have since reflected that the whole business would have been difficult for me without Edwards; I was intoxicated with high spirits, good conversation and beer in Calais. This was my first infidelity to the memory of Milan.

London made a very pleasant impression on me because of the walks one could take along the Thames towards *Little Chelsea*. There were little houses adorned with rose bushes there, which in my eyes had an authentically elegiac feel. It was the first time this insipid genre touched me.[*]

I can understand today[**] that I was still quite sick at soul. I had an almost rabid fear of any coarse person. The conversation of some coarse fat provincial merchant would stupefy me and make me unhappy for the rest of the entire day; for example, the rich banker Charles Durand of Grenoble who spoke to me in a friendly way. This disposition, which goes back to my childhood, and has given me so many black moments between the ages of fifteen and twenty-five, was forcefully re-emerging.

Secondly: I was so unhappy that I liked faces I knew. Any new face, which when I'm in good health keeps me entertained, then seemed importunate.

Chance brought me to Tavistock Hotel, Covent Garden. This is the hotel of the well-off people who come from the provinces to London.

[*] In five days, 20th–24th June 1832; I've reached this point, *id est* page 148. Rome, June 1832. Yesterday received a letter from Kashmir, June 1831, from V[ict]or Jacquemont.
[**] 24th June 1832.

My room, always left open in this country where you can steal with impunity, was eight feet wide and ten feet long. But, on the other hand, you ate lunch in a sitting-room maybe a hundred feet long, thirty wide and twenty high. There, you could eat[*] anything you wanted and as much as you wanted for fifty sous (two shillings). They would cook beefsteaks for you ad infinitum, or they would set before you a piece of roast beef weighing forty pounds together with a nice sharp knife. Then came the tea to help you digest all this meat. This room opened out in arches onto Covent Garden square. There I would find every day thirty or so fine Englishmen walking gravely along, many of them looking unhappy. There was none of the noisy affectation and fatuity of the French. This suited me; I was less unhappy in this sitting-room. Lunch always made me spend not an hour or two there just to pass the time, but a pleasant hour.

[*] 25th June [1832].

55

[Life of Henri Brulard[46], continued]

LIFE

2nd notebook from 151 to 270

[Continuation of the memoir of everything that happened to him during what he calls his last trip to Paris, from 21st June 1821 to 6th November 1830, when he went to Trieste as the French consul (For the beginning, see notebook No. 1, pages 1 to 150).]

I learnt to read mechanically the English newspapers, which basically didn't interest me. Later on, in 1826, I was really unhappy on this same Covent Garden square at the Ouxkum Hotel, or some equally uncouth name, in the opposite corner to Tavistock. Between 1826 and 1832, I met with no misfortunes.

There were no performances of Shakespeare the day I arrived in London; I went to Haymarket which, I seem to remember, was open. Despite the wretched atmosphere in the auditorium, I quite enjoyed myself.

She Stoops to Conquer, a comedy by ***, gave me a great deal of pleasure thanks to the performance of Jones, of the actor who played the husband of Miss ***, who indeed stooped to conquer: it's more or less the material of the *** by Marivaux. A young woman supposed to be married off disguises herself as a chambermaid.[47]

The Beaux' Stratagem I greatly enjoyed. During the day, I would wander round the outskirts of London; I'd often go to Richmond.

This famous terrace offers the same outlook as Saint-Germain-en-Laye. But the view looks down from a lower height perhaps across fields of charming green grass scattered with great trees venerable for their antiquity. All you can see from the top of the terrace at Saint-Germain, on the other hand, is dry, stony ground. Nothing equals this fresh greenery in England and the beauty of its trees: to cut them down would be a crime and a dishonour, while the minute he has the slightest need of money, a French landowner sells off the five or six great oaks standing in his grounds. The sight of Richmond, that of Windsor, reminded me of my dear Lombardy, the mountains of Brienza, Desio, Como, la Cadenabbia, the sanctuary of Varese, happy lands where my days of happiness were spent. I was so crazy in those moments of happiness that I have retained almost no distinct memory; at the most some date to mark, on a recently purchased book, the place where I'd read it. The least marginal comment means that if I ever reread this book, I can pick up the thread of my ideas and *take them further*. If I come up with no memories on rereading a book, the work has to be begun again.

One evening, sitting on the bridge at the foot of the Richmond terrace, I was reading the *Memoirs* of Mme Hutchinson[48]; this is one of my passions. – 'Mister Bell!' said a man stopping right in front of me.

It was M. B*** whom I'd met in Italy at Milady Jersey's. M. B***, a very astute man of about fifty, although he didn't exactly belong to the highest society, was nonetheless admitted to it (in England the classes are marked, as they are in India, the land of pariahs; see the Indian Cottage[49]).

'Have you seen Lady Jersey?' – 'No; I didn't know her that well in Milan and you English travellers are said to be rather prone to lose your memories when you come back across the Channel.' – 'What an idea! Go and see her.' – 'To be received coldly, or merely not to be recognised, would give me much more pain than the pleasure that even the most assiduous welcome would afford me.' – 'You haven't seen MM. Hobhouse[50], Brougham?' Same reply.

M. B*** who was as active as a diplomat, asked me for detailed news of France. – 'The younger middle-class generation, well brought-up and not knowing how to make room for themselves, find the protégés of the Congrégation[51] everywhere blocking their path; they will overthrow the Congrégation and, if possible, the Bourbons.' (As this sounds like a prediction, I leave the gentle reader every liberty not to believe it.) I have set this sentence here to add that my extreme distaste for every-thing I was talking about apparently gave me that air of unhappiness without which you are not esteemed in England.

When M. B.*** learnt that I knew M. de La Fayette, and M. de Tracy:

'Well!' he said in tones of the greatest astonishment, '*you haven't given your stay here all the importance you could have done!*'

'You could easily, had you wished, have gone to dine twice a week at Lord Holland's, Lady N***'s, Lady ***'s…'

'I didn't even tell people in Paris I was coming to London. I have only one aim in view: to see Shakespeare's plays performed.'

When M. B*** had understood what I meant, he thought I'd gone mad. The first time I went to the *Almack* ball, my banker, seeing my admission ticket, said to me with a sigh, 'I have been labouring for twenty-two years, Monsieur, to go to this ball, and *you* will be there in an hour's time!'

As society is divided up into sections like a bamboo, a man's main preoccupation is to rise into the class above his own, and all the efforts of this class go into preventing him from rising.

I have found these social conditions in France only once. It was when the generals of Napoleon's former army who had sold themselves to Louis XVIII were trying by base flattery to get themselves admitted into the salon of Mme de Talaru and others in the *Faubourg* Saint-Germain[52]. The humiliations that these vile creatures had to swallow every day would fill fifty pages. Poor Amédée de Pastoret, if he were ever to write his memoirs, would have many a fine tale to tell. Well, I don't think that the young men who are studying law in 1832 have it in themselves to put up with such humiliations. They'll commit a base act, or even do something wicked, if you like, if it can be done in a single day, but to allow themselves to be assassinated by the pinpricks of contempt is something that quite goes against the nature of anyone who wasn't born in the salons of 1780, which came back to life from 1804 to 1830.

This baseness, which will put up with everything from the wife of someone decorated with the Blue Ribbon (Mme de Talaru), will no longer be much in evidence except among young men born in Paris. And Louis-Philippe is not yet a subst[ant]ial enough figure for such salons to form in Paris, now or for a long time to come.

Probably the Reform Bill (June 1832) will bring to a halt in England the manufacture of men such as M. B***, who never forgave me for not having given my stay as much *importance* as I could have done. In 1821 I never suspected an objection that I realised on my 1826 trip: the dinners and balls given by the aristocracy cost a fantastic amount, and it's money which couldn't possibly be worse spent.

I owed particular thanks to M. B***: he taught me to return from Richmond to London by boat; it's a delightful trip.

Finally, on the *** 1821, they put up posters advertising *Othello* played by Kean. I was almost trampled in the rush to get my ticket for the pit. The time I spent waiting in the queue made me remember vividly the happy days of my youth when we got caught in the crush in 1800 to see Pinto's first performance (Germinal VIII)[53]. The unfortunate man who wants a ticket for Covent Garden is forced into narrow winding passages, only three feet wide, and lined with wooden walls that the friction from the clothes of those patiently waiting has worn down until they are perfectly smooth.

With my head full of literary ideas, it was only when I was already trapped in those dreadful corridors, and rage had given me a strength greater than that of my neighbours, that I said to myself, 'I'm not going to enjoy anything this evening. How stupid of me not to have bought a box ticket in advance!'

Fortunately, hardly had we reached the pit than the people who I'd been jostling against looked at me with good-natured and frank expressions. We exchanged a few well-meaning words on our past torments*; now I was no longer in a rage, I could concentrate entirely on my admiration for Kean, whom I knew only through the hyperboles of my travelling companion Edward Edwards. It appears that Kean is a hero from the backstreets, a man quite without elegance.

I could easily forgive him. If he'd been born wealthy or into a family of [?] any elegance, he wouldn't be Kean, but some frigid, conceited actor. The politeness of the upper classes in France, and probably England, *proscribes all energy*, and grinds it down if by chance it exists. Perfectly polite and perfectly devoid of all energy – that's the person I expect to see when they announce, at M. de Tracy's, M. de Syon or any other young man from the *Faubourg* Saint-Germain. And even then, I wasn't in any position in 1821 to judge of the complete insignificance of these enfeebled characters. M. de Syon, who comes to General La Fayette's home, and who followed him, I believe, to America, must be a monster of energy in the salon of Mme de La Trémoille.

Good God! How is it possible to be so insignificant! How can one

* 25th June [1832].

depict such people! All questions I asked myself during the winter of 1830, as I studied these young men. At the time their great preoccupation was the fear that their hair, arranged in such a way as to form a prominent wave from one side of their forehead to the other, wouldn't flop down.

For me.[54] I am discouraged by the absolute lack of dates. Imagination wears itself out chasing dates instead of imagining things.

My pleasure, on seeing Kean, was mingled with a great deal of surprise. The English, a *bilious* people, have very different gestures from ours to express the same movements of soul.

Baron de Lussinge and the excellent Barot came to join me in London; perhaps Lussinge had gone with me. I have an unfortunate talent for communicating my tastes; often, in speaking about my mistresses to my friends, I've made the latter fall in love with the former, or, what's even worse, I've made my mistress fall in love with the friend I really loved. This is what happened in the case of Mme Azur and Mérimée. It reduced me to despair for four days. As my despair lessened, I went to ask Mérimée to spare me this pain for a fortnight. 'For fifteen months,' he replied, 'I have lost any liking for her I once had. I saw her stockings creased on her legs (like a real slattern, a *garaude* as they say in the French of Grenoble).'

Barot, who does things rationally and sensibly, like a trader, persuaded us to take a courier. He was a conceited little Englishman. I despise them more than I do the others; fashion with them isn't a pleasure, but a serious duty which can't be neglected. I was able to judge sensibly anything that was unrelated to certain memories; I felt on the spot how ridiculous it is for the English worker to have to labour for eighteen hours. The poor Italian in his ragged clothes is much closer to happiness. He has time to make love, he gives himself up eighty or a hundred days of the year to a religion that is all the more entertaining in that it frightens him a bit, etc., etc.

My companions mocked me harshly. My paradox is turning into a truth under our very eyes, and will be a commonplace in 1840. My companions decided I was completely crazy when I added, 'The exorbitant and exhausting labour endured by the English worker avenges us for Waterloo and four coalitions. We at least have buried our dead, and our survivors are happier than the English.' All their lives long Barot and Lussinge will think I'm a rebel. Ten years on, I try to make them feel ashamed. 'Today you think the same way as I did in London in 1821.' They deny it, and I'm stuck with my reputation as a rebel. You can just imagine what happened to me when I had the misfortune to talk literature. My cousin Colomb for a long time thought I was really *envious*, because I told him that the *Lascaris* of M. Villemain was so boring the reader could hardly stay awake. And good God, just think what it was like when I tackled general principles! One day that I was talking about English labour, the conceited little man who was acting as our courier claimed his national honour had been offended. 'You're right,' I said to him, 'but we're feeling rather unhappy: we've run out of agreeable acquaintances.' – 'Monsieur, just leave it to me. I'll sort it all out for you myself… Don't ask anyone else, they'd rob you blind, etc., etc.'

My friends were laughing. In this way, so as to make fun of this conceited little man's honour, I found myself committed to a visit to the whores. There's nothing more grim and repellent than the details of the haggling our man made us go through the following day as he showed us the sights of London.

To begin with, our young ladies lived in a district at the back of beyond, Westminster Road, admirably placed for four sailor pimps to be able to give Frenchmen a drubbing. When we mentioned this to an English friend, he said, 'Stay away! It's a trap!' The conceited courier added that he'd haggled for ages so we'd have tea in the morning when we got up. The girls were reluctant to grant their favours and their tea for twenty-one shillings (twenty-five francs, five sous). But finally they'd agreed. Two or three Englishmen told us, 'An Englishman would never walk into a trap like that. Do you realise they'll take you a good league away from London?' We decided we wouldn't go. When the evening came, Barot looked at me. I understood his glance. 'We're strong,' I said to him, 'we have weapons.' Lussinge never dared to come.

Barot and I took a hackney carriage, and crossed Westminster Bridge. Then the cab drove us into streets without houses, between the gardens. Barot was laughing. 'If you were so brilliant with Alexandrine in a charming house in the centre of Paris, how do you think you'll perform here?' I had taken a profound dislike to the whole thing; if it weren't for the boredom of the after-dinner period in London when the theatres aren't open, as was the case on that day, and without the stimulus of possible danger, Westminster Road would never have seen me. Finally, having been two or three times on the point of overturning his coach in what claimed to be streets, despite being unpaved as I remember, the cab-driver, swearing, brought us to a halt outside a three-storey house which in its entirety can't have been more than twenty-five feet high. In all my life I have never seen anything so small.

Certainly, without the idea of danger, I'd never have gone in; I was expecting to see three horrid sluts. They were tiny, three young girls with lovely chestnut hair, a little timid, very assiduous, extremely pale.

The furniture was quite ridiculously small. Barot is big and fat, and I am fat, we couldn't find anywhere to sit, properly speaking, the furniture seemed made for dolls. We were frightened of breaking it. Our young girls saw our embarrassment; theirs only grew. We absolutely couldn't think what to say. Luckily Barot had the bright idea of talking about the garden.

'Oh! We've got a garden!' they said, not with pride but with a certain joy at finally having an object of luxury to show us. We went down into the garden with candles so we could see it; it was twenty-five feet long and ten wide. Barot and I burst out laughing. We saw there all the instruments of household economy owned by these poor girls: their little washtub for the clothes, their little vat with an elliptical apparatus for brewing their own beer.

I was touched and Barot disgusted. He said to me in French, 'Let's pay them and scarper.' – 'They'll be so humiliated,' I said. – 'Bah! Humiliated! You know what they're like. They'll send out for other customers, if it's not too late, or for their lovers, if they order things here the same way they do in France.'

These truths made no impression on me. Their poverty, all that little furniture, so clean and old, had touched me. We hadn't finished drinking our tea when I was on an intimate enough footing with them to confide to them in bad English our fear of being murdered. This completely disconcerted them. 'But anyway,' I added, 'the proof that we're doing you justice is that I'm telling you all this.'

We sent our conceited courier away. Then it was just as if I was with tender friends whom I was seeing again after a year-long trip.

None of the doors would close: this was another source of suspicion when we went off to bed. But what would have been the use of doors and strong locks? A single blow of the fist would have been enough to break through any of the little brick partitions. You could hear everything in this house. Barot, who had gone up to the second floor in the bedroom above mine, shouted out to me, 'If anyone tries to murder you, call me!'

I wanted to keep the light on; the modesty of my new lady friend, in every other way so docile and kind, refused to agree. She recoiled in obvious fear when she saw me setting out pistols and dagger on the night-table next to the bed on the side opposite the door. She was charming, small, well-proportioned, pale.

Nobody murdered us. The next day we decided that as they had served us tea, it was our turn, and we sent the courier to find Lussinge, urging him to come over with some cold meat and wine. He soon appeared, escorted by an excellent lunch, and quite astonished at our enthusiasm.

The two sisters sent for one of their girlfriends.* We left them some wine and some cold meat, the beauty of which seemed to surprise those poor girls.

They thought we were making fun of them when we told them we'd be returning. Miss ***, my friend, took me aside and told me, 'I wouldn't go out if I could hope that you'd come back this evening. But our house is too poor for people like you.'

The whole day long, I could only think about the nice, cosy, quiet evening (*full of snugness*[55]) that lay ahead of me. The play seemed to drag on. Barot and Lussinge wanted to see all the bold young ladies who thronged the foyer at Covent Garden. Finally, Barot and I arrived at our little house. When those damsels saw us unpacking bottles of claret and champagne, the poor girls gazed with wide-eyed astonishment. I could easily believe that they had never found themselves opposite an unopened bottle of *real Champaign*.

Fortunately the cork in our bottle popped; they were perfectly

* 26th June [1832]. Church of S. Giovanni dei Fiorentini.

63

happy, but their transports were restrained and decent. Nothing could have been more decent than the whole way they behaved. We already knew as much.

This was the first real, intimate consolation for the unhappiness that poisoned all my moments of solitude. It's obvious that I was only twenty years old, in 1821. If I'd really been thirty-eight, as my baptismal certificate seemed to prove, I could have tried to find this consolation with the honest women of Paris who showed me some sympathy. However, I sometimes doubt that I'd have succeeded. What is called a 'high-society' manner, and means that Mme de Marnier has a different manner from Mme Edwards, often seems to me to be a damnable affectation and for a moment it seals my heart hermetically.

This is one of my greatest misfortunes, do you feel it in the same way as I do? I'm mortally shocked by the tiniest nuances.

A little more or a little less of the manner of high society makes me exclaim to myself, '*What a bourgeois woman!*' or '*What a dummy from the Faubourg Saint-Germain!*' and, from that very instant, I am left with nothing more than distaste or *irony* in the service of my neighbour.

One can know everything, except oneself: 'I am far from thinking that I know everything,' as a polite man from the noble *faubourg* would add, taking good care to protect all avenues from the attack of ridicule. My doctors, whenever I've been ill, have always treated me with pleasure, considering me to be a monster, for my excessive *nervous irritability*. Once, a window open in the room next door whose door was closed made me feel cold. The least smell (except for bad smells) weakens my arm and my left leg and makes me feel as if I'm about to fall on that side.

But all these details are the most abominable egotism! – Doubtless, and what else is this book* but an abominable piece of egotism? What's the use of putting on a display of pedantic grace like M. Villemain in an article yesterday on the arrest of M. de Chateaubriand?

If this book is boring, in two years' time it will be wrapping up butter at the grocer's; if it's not boring, people will see that egotism, *so long as it's sincere*, is one way of depicting that human heart in the

* 30th June [1832]. Two days without work. Official business has kept me busy.

knowledge of which we have made giant strides since 1721, the period of the *Persian Letters* of that great man I have studied so deeply, Montesquieu.

The progress is sometimes so astonishing that Montesquieu appears coarse in comparison.*

I found myself in such good spirits thanks to my stay in London and the fact that I could spend the whole evening being jocund, in bad English, that I let the Baron head back to Paris, where his office work summoned him, and Barot, summoned by his Baccarat and carding machine business. And yet I greatly enjoyed their company. We didn't talk about the fine arts, which has always been my stumbling-block with my friends. The English are, I think, the most obtuse and most barbarous race in the whole world. So much so that I can forgive them for their infamous behaviour at St-Helena.

They didn't even feel it. To be sure, a Spaniard, an Italian, even a German would have imagined the martyrdom of Napoleon. Those honest English, always skirting the abyss of the risk of starvation if they forget for an instant to work, dismissed the idea of St-Helena, just as they dismiss the idea of Raphael, as being prone to make them *waste their time*, and that's all there is to be said about it.

Between the three of us – me for daydreaming and my knowledge of Say and (Adam) Smith[56], the Baron de Lussinge for seeing the bad side in everything, and Barot for work (which transforms a pound of steel worth twelve francs into three quarters of a pound of springs for watches, worth ten thousand francs), we comprised a pretty complete traveller.

When I was alone, the honest respectability of the English family which has an income of ten thousand francs fought in my heart against the complete demoralisation of the Englishman who, having expensive tastes, has realised that in order to satisfy them he must sell himself to the government. The English Philippe de Ségur is for me at one and

* Writing this makes me happy. Official work has kept me busy in one way or another day and night for three days (June 1832). I wouldn't be able to take up again at four o'clock, once my letters to ministers were all signed and sealed, a work of the imagination. I can do this easily, without any other painful effort or plan than that of *remembering*.

the same time the vilest of people and the one most absurd to have to listen to.

I left like *** without knowing, because of the conflict between these two ideas, whether it was necessary to hope for some *Terror* which would cleanse the stables of Augeas in England.

The poor girl at whose home I spent my evenings assured me that she would eat apples and would cost me nothing if I would take her to France with me.

I was harshly punished for advising a sister I had that she should come to Milan in 1816, I think. Mme Périer stuck to me like a limpet, burdening me forever with the responsibility for her fate.[57] Mme Périer had all the virtues and sufficient good sense and amiability. I was forced to quarrel with her to deliver myself from this limpet that was annoyingly stuck to the hull of my vessel, and who willy-nilly was making me responsible for all her future happiness. Dreadful business!

It was this alarming idea that prevented me from taking Miss Appleby to Paris. I would have avoided many a moment of diabolical gloom. For my misfortune, as affectation is so hateful to me, it's difficult for me to be simple, sincere, kind – in a word perfectly German – with a Frenchwoman.

(I'll make this article on London in 1821 longer when I find my English plays with the dates of the days on which I saw them performed.)

One day, it was announced that eight poor devils were to be executed. To my eyes, when they hang a thief or a murderer in England, it's the aristocracy which is sacrificing a victim to its own security, for it's the aristocracy which has forced him to be a villain, etc., etc. This truth, so paradoxical today, will perhaps be a commonplace when people read my ramblings.

I spent the night telling myself that it's the traveller's duty to see such spectacles and the effect they have on the race that has stayed true to its roots (*who has raciness*[58]). The following day, when I was awoken at eight o'clock, it was pouring with rain. The thing I was trying to force myself to do was so painful for me that I still remember the inner struggle. I didn't go to see that atrocious spectacle.

CHAPTER SEVEN

On my return to Paris, towards the end of December, it so happened that I was able to take a little more interest in men and things. Today I can see that this was because I knew that, independently of what I had left behind in Milan, I would now be able to find a little happiness, or at least amusement, elsewhere. This elsewhere was the little house of Miss Appleby.

But I didn't have enough common sense to arrange my life systematically. Chance continued to guide my relationships. For example:

There was once a War Minister in Naples by the name of Micheroux. This poor officer of fortune was, if I remember, from Liège. He left to his two sons pensions at Court; at Naples, people count on the grace and favour of the king as on a common inheritance.

The Chevalier Alexandre Micheroux used to dine at the table d'hôte at No. 47, rue de Richelieu. He's a handsome lad with the phlegmatic appearance of a Dutchman. He was consumed by worries. At the time of the 1820 Revolution, he was peacefully ensconced in Naples, and a royalist.

Francesco, the prince royal and since then the most despised of *Kings*[59], was the regent and special protector of the Chevalier de M[icheroux]. He summoned him and asked him, addressing him familiarly, to accept the post as minister in Dresden, something the apathetic Miche[roux] wasn't in the slightest interested in. However, as he wasn't brave enough to displease a Royal Highness and hereditary prince, he went to Dresden. Soon Francesco exiled him, condemned him to death, if I remember, or at least confiscated his allowances.

Not being a man of wit or having any particular talent, the chevalier was his own tormentor: for a long time he worked for eighteen hours a day, like an Englishman, so as to become a painter, musician, metaphysician, heaven knows what. This education was so directed as if to cohere with his sense of logic.

I know all about his astonishing work rate from an actress friend of mine who, from her window, would see this handsome young man work from 5 a.m. until 5 p.m. at his painting, and then spend the whole evening reading. From these terrible labours the chevalier had been left with the art of accompanying someone at the piano in a very superior fashion, and enough good sense or musical good taste, as you prefer, not to be entirely taken in by the whipped cream and braggadocio of Rossini. As soon as he wanted to discuss things seriously, this not very bright fellow, overwhelmed by false learning, fell prey to the most comic stupidity. In politics, especially, he was curious. Besides, I've never known anything more poetic and absurd than the liberal Italian or Carbonaro who, from 1821 to 1830, filled the liberal salons in Paris.[60]

One evening after dinner Mi[cheroux] went up to his room. Two hours later, when we didn't see him come to the Café de Foy where one of us who had wasted his coffee was paying for it, we went up to see him. We found him almost unconscious with pain. He was suffering from *scolozione*[61]; after dinner, the local pain had increased; this phlegmatic and melancholy man had started to consider all his troubles, including money troubles. The pain had overwhelmed him. Another man would have killed himself; as for him, he would have been content with dying unconscious if we hadn't with great difficulty woken him up.

This destiny touched me. Perhaps partly through the reflection: 'Here is a man, after all, who is more unhappy than me.' Barot lent him five hundred francs which were returned. The next day Lussinge or I introduced him to Mme Pasta.

A week later, we realised that he was now her favourite friend. There was nothing colder and more reasonable than the way those two people treated each other. I saw them every day for four or five years; I wouldn't have been surprised after all that time if a magician, granting me the power of invisibility, had put me in a position to see that they didn't make love together, but were simply talking about music. I am sure that Mme Pasta, who for eight or ten years didn't merely live in Paris, but set the fashion there for a good three quarters of this time, never had a French lover.*

At the time when we introduced M[icheroux] to her, the handsome Lagrange would come every evening to spend three hours boring us

---

* 30th June 1832, *written*[62] twelve pages at the end of an evening, after doing my official tasks. I would never have been able to labour like this on a work of the imagination.

stiff, sitting next to her on her sofa. It was this general who played the role of Apollo or the handsome Spaniard delivered from captivity in the ballets of the Imperial Court. I have seen Queen Caroline Murat and the divine Princess Borgese dancing dressed up as savages with him. He was one of the most empty people in polite society, to be sure; and that's saying a lot.

Since it is much more of a fateful mistake for a young man to drop some unseemly remark than it is to his advantage to say something clever, posterity, probably less inane, will have no idea of how insipid polite society was.

The Chevalier Missirini[63] had distinguished, almost elegant manners. In this regard, he formed a perfect contrast with Lussinge and even Barot*, who is merely a fine and stout-hearted provincial lad who, by chance, has earned millions of francs. The elegant manners of Missirini attached me to him. I soon realised that he was a perfectly cold-hearted man.

He had learnt music in the same way that a scholar from the Academy of Inscriptions learns or pretends to learn Persian. He had *learnt* to admire such and such a piece, the first quality always lay in a sound that was just right, in a phrase that was perfectly correct.

In my view, the first quality, by far, is that of being *expressive*.

The first quality, for me, in everything set down black on white, is that of being able to say with Boileau:

Whether good, whether bad, my poem always makes sense.[64]

As the friendship between Missirini and Mme Pasta grew ever closer, I went to find lodgings on the third floor of the Hôtel des Lillois, of which that good woman occupied successively the second and the first floor.

She was, in my eyes, without vices, without failings, a simple, even-tempered, equitable, natural character, and she had the greatest tragic talent I have ever known.

Out of a young man's habit (remember that I was only twenty in 1821), I would first of all have liked her to feel love for me, who so greatly

* 1st July 1832.

69

admired her. Today I can see that she was too cold, too reasonable, not wild enough, not caressing enough for our relationship, if there had been enough love in it, to continue. It would have been a mere passing fancy on my part; she would quite understandably have been indignant, and would have broken it off. So it's better that things remained on the level of the holiest and most devout friendship on my side, while she kept to a feeling of the same nature, albeit with its ups and downs.

Missirini, being a little afraid of me, loaded two or three fine slanders onto me: I *used them all up* by not paying them the slightest attention. After six or eight months, I suppose Mme Pasta said to herself, 'There isn't a shred of common sense in the fellow!'

But something always lingers on, though, after six or eight years, these slanders have resulted in our friendship becoming perfectly calm. I've never felt a moment's anger against Missirini. After the royal treatment he received from François, he could have said, like I forget which of Voltaire's heroes:

A noble poverty is all I still possess[65]

and I suppose that *la Giuditta*, as we called her in Italian, used to lend him a few small sums to protect him from the worst slings and arrows of that poverty.

I wasn't all that witty in those days, but there were already people jealous of me. M. de Perrey, the spy from the circle of M. de Tracy, knew about my friendly relationship with Mme Pasta: those people find out everything from their friends. He presented it so it would seem most hateful in the eyes of the ladies of the rue d'Anjou. The most decent woman, the one to whose mind any idea of a relationship is as foreign as possible, can't forgive the idea of a relationship with an actress. This had already happened to me in Marseilles in 1805; but then, Mme Séraphie T*** was right not to wish to see me every evening when she discovered my relationship with Mlle Louason (that woman who was so witty, who has since become Mme de Barkoff).

In the rue d'Anjou, which, basically, formed my most respectable circle of acquaintances, not even old M. de Tracy, the philosopher, ever forgave me for my relationship with an actress.

I am animated, passionate, wild, and sincere to excess in friendship and in love, until the first cooling off. Then, from the wildness of a sixteen year old I pass, in the twinkling of an eye, to the machiavellianism of a fifty year old and, after a week, there's nothing left but *melting ice*, a perfect chilliness. (This has just happened to me recently again, *with Lady*[66] Angelica, 1832, May.)

I was at the point of giving the Tracy circle all the friendship in my heart, when I noticed a sprinkling of hoar-frost on the surface. From 1821 to 1830, I stopped behaving there in any other than a cold and machiavellian – that is, perfectly prudent – way. I can still see the broken stems of several budding friendships that were at the point of being formed in the rue d'Anjou. The excellent Countess de Tracy, whom I reproach myself bitterly for not having loved more, did not reciprocate this hint of coldness. And yet I was coming back from England for her, with an openness of heart, and the need to be the sincere friend of someone (which calmed down by pure *consenso*), while resolving to be cold and calculating with everyone else in the salon.

In Italy, I adored the opera. The sweetest moments in my life, without compare, all occurred in opera-houses. By dint of being happy in *la Scala* (the Milan opera-house), I had become a kind of connoisseur.

At the age of ten, my father, who had all the prejudices of religion and aristocracy, vehemently prevented me from studying music. At sixteen, I learnt successively to play the violin, to sing, and to play the clarinet. Only in this last way did I manage to produce sounds which gave me pleasure. My music teacher, a kind, good-looking German by the name of Hermann, made me play tender cantilenas. Who knows? Perhaps he knew Mozart? This was in 1797, Mozart had just died.

But that great name had not at the time been revealed to me. A great passion for mathematics swept me away; for two years, my only thoughts were for maths. I left for Paris, where I arrived the day after 18th Brumaire (10th November [17]99)[67]. Since then, whenever I've wanted to study music, I've found that it was too late by this sign: my passion would lessen in proportion as I learnt a little more about it. The sounds I made filled me with repugnance, quite differently from so many fourth-rate performers who owe their little scrap of talent, which all the same can give pleasure on evenings in the country, to the intrepid way they make their instruments grate on their own ears in the mornings. But they don't find that the noise grates, because… This metaphysics could be prolonged forever.

Anyway, I adored music and it gave me the greatest happiness from 1806 to 1810 in Germany. From 1814 to 1821 in Italy. In Italy I could talk music with old Mayer, with young Pacini, with the composers. The performers, Marquis Carafa, Viscontini of Milan, felt on the other hand that I didn't have any common sense. It's just as if today I talked politics with a sous-préfet.

One of the things that most astonished Count Daru, an authentic man of letters from top to toe, worthy of the stupefaction of the Academy of Inscriptions in 1828, was that I was capable of writing a page that could give pleasure to someone. One day he bought from Delaunay, who told me, a little book of mine which, as it was out of print, was being sold at forty francs. His astonishment was enough to make you die laughing, said the bookseller.

'What! forty francs!' – 'Yes, Monsieur le Comte, and you're lucky, and you'll do the seller a favour if you don't take it at that price.' – 'Is it possible!' said the academician, raising his eyes heavenwards; 'that boy! As ignorant as a carp!'

He was speaking in all good faith. People who live in the antipodes, looking at the moon when it is merely a slender crescent for us, say to themselves, 'What an admirable glow! The moon is almost full!' Count Daru, member of the French Academy, associate member of the Academy of Sciences, etc., etc., and I viewed the heart of man, nature, etc., from opposite sides.

One of the things so admired by Missirini, whose attractive room was next door to mine, on the second floor of the Hôtel des Lillois, was that there were people prepared to listen to me when I talked music. He couldn't get over his surprise when he realised it was I who had written a little book about Haydn. He quite approved of the book, 'too metaphysical,' he said; but that *I* could have written it, that *I* could have been its author, when I am incapable of striking a diminished seventh on a piano, that was something that made him stare in wide-eyed astonishment. And he had very nice eyes, when by chance he put a little expression into them.

This astonishment, which I've just described rather long-windedly, is something I encountered, to a greater or lesser extent, on the part of all the people I spoke to until the period (1827) when I started to be witty.

I'm like a respectable woman who becomes a whore, I need to overcome at every moment the modesty of a respectable man who hates talking about himself. This book has done nothing else, however. I didn't foresee it would turn out like this, perhaps it will make me drop the whole thing. The only difficulty I foresaw was having the courage to tell the truth about everything: this is the least of my problems.

I lack quite a few details on these distant periods; I'll become less dry and even verbose as I approach the interval between 1826 and 1830. Then, my unhappiness forced me to become witty; I can remember it all as if it were yesterday.

Because of an unfortunate physical disposition which has led to me being treated as a liar, an eccentric and above all a bad Frenchman, I find it very difficult to derive any pleasure from music sung in a French concert room.

My main preoccupation, as was that of all my friends in 1821, was nonetheless the opera buffa.

Mme Pasta was performing *Tancred*, *Othello*, *Romeo and Juliet*… in a way that not only has never been equalled, but had certainly never been foreseen by the composers of those operas.

Talma, whom posterity will perhaps laud to the skies, had a tragic soul, but he was so stupid that he fell into the most ridiculous affectations. I suspect that, over and beyond the total eclipse of intelligence, he still had that servility indispensable to make a successful start – something I was so pained to come across even in the admirable and likeable Béranger.

So Talma was probably servile, base, a creep, a flatterer, etc., and, perhaps, something even worse towards Mme de Staël who, continuously and stupidly preoccupied by her ugliness, too (if a word such as stupid can be applied to that admirable woman), needed palpable and ever-renewed reasons to be *reassured*.

Mme de Staël, who had admirably mastered, like one of her lovers,

Prince Talleyrand, *the art of success in Paris*, realised* that she had everything to win by giving her seal of approval to Talma's success, which was starting to become widespread and to lose, thanks to its durability, its somewhat unrespectable character as a mere *fashion*.**

Talma's success started out as boldness; he had enough courage to innovate, the only kind of courage surprising in France. He was completely new in Voltaire's *Brutus* and shortly afterwards in that poor piece of derivative exaggeration, the *Charles IX* of M. de Chénier.

An old and very bad actor that I knew, the boring royalist Naudet, was so shocked at the innovative genius of the young Talma, that he several times provoked him to a duel. I don't know, in fact, where Talma had found the idea and the courage to innovate; I saw him completely failing to rise to that level.

Despite his coarse, artificial voice and the almost equally annoying affectation of his dislocated wrists, anyone in France disposed to feel moved at the fine tragic sentiments of the third act of Ducis' *Hamlet* or the fine scenes in the last acts of *Andromaque* had no other resource than to see Talma.

He had a tragic soul, and to an astonishing degree. If he had joined to it a simple personality and the courage to ask for advice, he could have gone really far; for example, as sublime as Monvel in Auguste (*Cinna*). I'm here speaking entirely of things I've seen and seen properly or at least in great detail, having been a passionate devotee of the Théâtre-Français.

A writer and man of wit, who often spoke in public (the Abbé Geoffroy), amused himself by trying to destroy Talma's reputation. Fortunately for Talma, Mme de Staël had seen fit to laud him to the skies. This eloquent woman took on the responsibility of teaching the foolish in what terms they should speak of Talma. It is easy to guess that she did not refrain from overblown words. Talma's name spread through Europe.

His abominable affectation became more and more invisible to the French, that race of sheep. I'm not a sheep, and this means I'm nothing at all.

* In 1803, perhaps. Check.
** 1st July 1832.

The vague melancholy imposed by destiny, as in *Oedipus*, will never have an actor comparable to Talma. In Manlius, he was really Roman: '*Take, read*,' and: '*Do you recognise the hand of Rutilius?*' were divine. This is because there was no means of inserting the abominable singsong of alexandrines. What a nerve I must have had to think that in 1805! I almost shudder to write such blasphemies today (1832) now that the two idols have fallen. However, in 1805, I was already predicting 1832, and success astonishes me and *stupefies me (Cinna)*.

Will the same thing happen in the case of the ***[68]?

The continuous singsong, the coarse voice, the flutter of the wrists, the affected gait stopped me enjoying five minutes' uninterrupted pleasure in seeing Talma. At every instant, I had to choose, a wretched occupation for the imagination (or rather, the mind kills off the imagination). The only thing that was perfect in Talma was his facial expression and his *vacant gaze*. I'll come back to these words of wisdom with regard to the madonnas of Raphael and Mlle Virginie de La Fayette (Mme Adolphe Perier) who had this great beauty to a supreme degree and of which her good grandmother, Countess de Tracy, was really proud.

I found the tragic sense that suited me in Kean and I adored him. He filled my eyes and my heart. I can still see, there in front of me, Richard III and Othello.

But the tragic sense in a woman, where for me it is at its most touching, I have found only in Mme Pasta and there it was pure, perfect, unmixed. At her home, she was silent and impassive. In the evenings, for two hours she was… When she returned home, she spent two hours on her sofa weeping and having an attack of nerves.

And yet this tragic talent was mixed with a talent for singing. The ear brought to perfection the emotion that had started with the eyes, and Mme Pasta would remain for a long time, for instance two or three seconds, in the same position. Did this make things easier, or was it one more obstacle to overcome? I've often pondered the question. I incline to think that this circumstance of remaining perforce in the same position for a long time neither makes things easier nor more difficult. Mme Pasta's soul still has to confront the difficulty of focusing her attention on singing well.

Chevalier Missirini, Lussinge, di Fiori, Sutton Sharpe and several others of us, all united in our admiration for the *gran donna*, had an eternal topic of conversation in the way she had played in the last performance of *Romeo*, and in the stupid remarks made on that occasion by those poor French men of letters, obliged to have an opinion on something so antipathetic to the French character: *music*. Abbé Geoffroy, far and away the wittiest and most learned of journalists, made no bones about calling Mozart a *Tin-pan Alley composer*; he was in good faith and could only enjoy Grétry and Monsigny, whom he'd *learnt*.

I beg you, gentle reader, understand these words. They contain the history of music in France.

Just imagine the asinine comments that the whole rabble of men of letters, journalists so inferior to M. Geoffroy, came out with in 1822. The reviews of this witty schoolmaster have been collected, and they are said to form a dull collection. They were divine when they were served up in an improvised fashion, twice a week, and a thousand times superior to the heavy-handed articles of a M. Hoffmann or a M. Féletz which, when collected, cut a better figure perhaps than Geoffroy's delightful reviews. In their time, I would have lunch at the Café Hardy that was then fashionable with delicious broiled kidneys. Well, the days when there wasn't a review by Geoffroy, I didn't enjoy my lunch.

He'd write his reviews while listening to his pupils reading out their Latin proses at the *** boarding-school where he was a master. One day, when he took some of his pupils into a café near the Bastille for a beer, they had the great pleasure of coming across a newspaper that told them what their master did: they'd often see him writing, holding the paper right up to his nose, he was so short-sighted.

It was thanks to his short-sightedness that Talma had developed that vacant gaze which shows so much soulfulness (like the inner half-concentration you fall into the minute there's nothing interesting to draw the attention outwards).

I feel that Mme Pasta's talent has diminished. She didn't find it very difficult* to play a great-souled person naturally: that's how she was.

For example, she was miserly, or, if you prefer, quite understandably

* 1st July 1832.

stingy, having as she did a spendthrift husband. Well, in a single month she managed to have two hundred francs distributed to some poor Italian refugees. And quite a few of them were far from gracious, quite enough to put anyone off acts of charity; for example, M. Giannone, the poet from Modena, whom heaven absolve. What a look he had!

M. di Fiori, who so resembles the *Jupiter Mansuetus* – they are as alike as two peas in a pod – condemned to death at the age of twenty-three in Naples in 1799, made himself responsible for distributing Mme Pasta's aid fairly. He was the only one to know and he told me a long time afterwards, in confidence. The Queen of France, in today's paper, has had recorded a charitable gift of seventy francs sent to an old woman (June 1832)!

CHAPTER EIGHT

Over and above the impudence of continually talking about oneself, this work presents another potential source of discouragement: how many bold things that I can only put forward in trembling will be common-place platitudes, ten years after my death, if, that is, heaven grants me a reasonably decent life span of eighty-four or ninety years!

On the other hand, there's a certain pleasure in talking about General Foy, Mme Pasta, Lord Byron, Napoleon, etc., and all those great men or at least those very distinguished people it has been my good fortune to know and who have deigned to talk with me!

Furthermore, if the reader is envious like my contemporaries, he should console himself: few of these great men I have so liked ever managed to read my character. I even think they found me more boring than another man; perhaps they saw me merely as a *sentimental fellow prone to exaggeration*.

This is the worst kind, after all. It's only since I developed my wit that I have been appreciated and far more than I deserve. General Foy, Mme Pasta, M. de Tracy, Canova, never *read into my character* (this stupid phrase 'read into my character' rankles) to find a soul filled with a rare kindness, I have the right *bump* for it (Gall's system)[69] and a fiery spirit capable of understanding them.

One of the men who never understood me and perhaps, all in all, the one I liked best (he was the realisation of my ideal, as I forget which overblown fool said) was Andrea Corner of Venice, the former aide-de-camp of Prince Eugene in Milan.

I was in 1811 the close friend of Count Widmann, captain of the company of guards in Venice (I was his mistress' lover). I again bumped into the amiable Widmann in Moscow where he asked me in even tones to make him a senator of the Kingdom of Italy. At the time, people thought I was the favourite of Count Daru, my cousin, who, on the contrary, never liked me. In 1811 Widmann introduced me to Corner who struck me as looking like a handsome figure from Paolo Veronese.

Count Corner has, it is said, run through five million francs. He performs actions of the rarest generosity* and the most completely

* 1st July [1832].

78

opposed to the character of the French man of the world. As for bravery, he has had the two crosses from the hand of Napoleon (Iron Cross and Legion of Honour).

It was he who said so naively at four in the evening, on the day of the Battle of the Moskva (7th September 1812), 'But this devil of a battle is never going to end!' Widmann or Migliorini told me the following day.

None of the Frenchmen, so brave but so affected, that I knew in the army at that time, for instance General Caulaincourt, General Montbrun, etc., would ever have dared say such a thing, not even the Duke of Friuli (Michel Duroc). And yet he was a man of such a rare nature, as far as personality goes, but for this quality as well as for amusing wit he was far from being an Andrea Corner.

This amiable man was then in Paris without any money, starting to turn bald. He didn't have any of the things he needed at the age of thirty-eight, when, if you are disabused, boredom starts to make its presence felt. Also, and this is the only failing I've ever seen in him, sometimes in the evenings he would go for a stroll by himself, a bit drunk, in the middle of the garden (then dark) of the Palais-Royal. Such is the end of all illustrious unhappy men: dethroned princes, M. Pitt seeing Napoleon's successes, and hearing the news of the Battle of Austerlitz.*

Lussinge,** the most prudent man I've ever known, in the desire to ensure he had someone to go for a stroll with him every morning, had the greatest reluctance to introduce me to anyone else.

Still, he took me to the home of M. de Maisonnette, one of the strangest people I've ever known in Paris. He is dark-complexioned, lean, very short, like a Spaniard, he has the same darting eye and testy bravery.

The fact that he can write in one evening thirty elegant and verbose pages to prove a political thesis following a prompting sent to him by the minister, at 6 p.m., before going off to dinner, is something that Maisonnette has in common with men like ***, Vitet, Léon Pillet,

* 1st July 1832. *They speak of* Lamb[ruschini] *as* La Bourdonnaye *secretary and of Sanctus Olai départure. Yesterday* Mme Malibran.[70]
** 2nd July 1832.

Saint-Marc-Girardin and other writers of the Treasury. The curious, the incredible thing, is that Maisonnette believes in what he writes. He has been successively in love, but in love to the point of sacrificing his life, with M. Decazes, then with M. de Villèle, then, I think, with M. de Martignac. At least the latter was a likeable man.

Many a time I have tried to read into Maisonnette's character. I thought I could detect a total absence of logic and sometimes a capitulation of conscience, the numbing effect of a twinge of remorse that was trying to express itself. All this founded on the great axiom, 'I have to live'.

Maisonnette has no idea of the duties of a citizen; he regards them as I regard the relations between men and angels as believed in so firmly by M. F. Ancillon, current Minister for Foreign Affairs in Berlin (some-one I knew well in 1806 and [180]7). Maisonnette is quite free of the duties of a citizen, just as Dominique is free of those of religion. If sometimes, as he so often writes the word *honour* and loyalty, he is afflicted by a twinge of remorse, he acquits himself of it in his heart of hearts through his chivalrous devotion to his friends. If I'd wanted to, after neglecting him out of boredom for six months in succession, I'd have made him get up at 5 a.m. to run errands for me. He'd have gone to the Pole in search of any man who had doubted his honour as a man of society, and fought a duel with him.

Never wasting his intelligence on utopian schemes for the public happiness, or on a rational constitution, [?] he was admirable when it came to knowing individual facts. One evening Lussinge, Gazul[71] and I were talking about M. de Jouy, then a fashionable author, Voltaire's successor; he rises to his feet and goes to look in one of his voluminous collections for the autograph letter in which M. de Jouy asked the Bourbons for the Cross of Saint-Louis. He didn't take two minutes to find this document, which clashed so comically with the fanatical virtue of the liberal M. de Jouy.

Maisonnette didn't have the cowardly and profound knavishness, the perfectly Jesuitical spirit, of the staff of the *Journal des Débats*. Thus, at the *Débats*, they were scandalised at the fifteen or twenty thousand francs that M. de Villèle, that very positive man, gave M[aisonne]tte.

The people of the rue des Prêtres regarded him as a ninny, and yet his salary kept them awake at nights, like the laurels of Miltiades[72].

When we had admired the letter of Jouy's adjutant-general, M[aisonne]tte said, 'It's strange that the two cheerleaders of contemporary literature and liberalism are both called Etienne'. M. de Jouy was born in Jouy; his father was a bourgeois by the name of Etienne. Endowed with that French effrontery* that the poor Germans simply cannot conceive of, at the age of fourteen young Etienne left Jouy near Versailles to go to India. There he had himself called Etienne de Jouy, E. de Jouy and finally just de Jouy. He really did become a captain; later on an agent, I think, made him a colonel. Although brave, he saw little if any service. He was a very handsome man. One day in India he and two or three friends went into a temple to escape the dreadful heat. There they found the priestess, a kind of Vestal Virgin. M. de Jouy found it amusing to make her unfaithful to Brahma on the very altar of her god.

The Indians realised what had happened, came running up in arms, cut the wrists and then the head off the vestal virgin, and cut in half the officer who was a chum of the author of *Sylla* who, after the death of his friend, managed to climb onto a horse and is still galloping.

Before M. de Jouy applied his talent for intrigue to literature, he was Secretary-General of the préfecture of Brussels around 1810. There, I think, he was the lover of the prefect's wife and the factotum of M. de Pontécoulant, the prefect, a man of real wit. Between them, M. de Jouy and he suppressed begging. Which is a huge achievement anywhere and more than anywhere in Belgium, an eminently Catholic country.

On the great man's fall, M. de Jouy asked for the cross of Saint-Louis; the imbeciles who were reigning refused his request, and he began making fun of them through literature and did more harm to them than any of the good done by all the men of letters of the *Débats*, so richly paid. See in 1820 the fury of the *Débats* against *la Minerve*[73].

M. de Jouy, thanks to his *Hermite de la Chaussée d'Antin*, a book so well adapted to the spirit of the bourgeois of France and the silly curiosity of the German, saw himself as, and *believed himself to be*, for five or six years, the successor of Voltaire whose bust he had, for that reason, in the garden of his house of Les Trois-Frères.

* 2nd July 1832.

Since 1829 the romantic littérateurs, who don't even have as much wit as M. de Jouy, pass him off as the *Cotin* of the period (Boileau), and his old age is made unhappy (*amareggiata*) by the extravagant fame of his maturity.[74]

He shared the dictatorship of the literary realm, when I arrived in 1821, with another and far coarser fool, M. A.-V. Arnault, of the Institute, the lover of Mme Brac. I saw this man a lot at the home of Mme de Cuvier, his mistress's sister. He had the wit of a drunken porter. Still, he wrote some nice poetry:

> *'Where are you going to, leaf from the oak tree?'*
> *'I'm going wherever the wind will blow me.'*

He wrote this the day before he left to go into exile. Personal un-happiness had given some life to that soul of cork. I had known him behaving very basely, very obsequiously, around 1811 at Count Daru's whom he received into the French Academy. M. de Jouy, a much nicer man, was selling the residues of his masculine beauty to Mme Davillier, the oldest and most boring of the coquettes of the period. She was, or still is, much more ridiculous than Countess Baraguey-d'Hilliers who, at the tender age of fifty-seven, recruited her lovers from among the men of wit. I don't know if it's for that reason that I was obliged to flee from her at Mme Dubignon's. She took that dullard Masson (rapporteur of the Council of State), and when one of my women friends said to her, 'What! Such an ugly man!' she replied, 'I took him for his wit.' The best thing is that the gloomy secretary of M. Beugnot had as much wit as beauty. He can't be denied the wit to behave properly, the art of advancing by his patience and swallowing insults, and, indeed, a certain knowledge, not of financial matters, but of the art of noting the way state finances operate. Simpletons confuse these two things. Mme d'Hilliers, whose arms I was gazing at – they were still superb – said to me, 'I'll teach you to make a fortune with your talents. Left to your own devices, you'll come a cropper.'

I didn't have enough wit to understand her. I would often look at this old Countess because of the charming Victorine dresses she wore[75]. I am crazy about a well-made dress, for me it is a profound pleasure.

Many years ago, Mme N.C.D. gave me this taste, linked to the delightful memories of Cideville.

It was, if I remember correctly, Mme Baraguey-d'Hilliers who told me that the author of a delightful song that I adored and had in my pocket wrote little verse compositions for the birthdays of those two old baboons: MM. de Jouy and Arnault and the horrid Mme Davillier. This is something I've never done, but then I've also never done

Le Roi d'Yvetot
Le Sénateur
La Grand-mère.[76]

M. de Béranger, pleased at having acquired, by flattering those two scarecrows, the title of great poet (so well deserved, indeed), disdained to flatter the government of Louis-Philippe to which so many liberals have sold themselves.

CHAPTER NINE

But I must go back to a little garden in the rue Caumartin. There, every evening in summer some nice bottles of chilled beer were waiting for us, poured out for us by a tall and beautiful woman, Mme Romance, separated from her husband, a rascally printer, and the mistress of M. de Maisonnette, who had bought her from the said husband for two or three thousand francs.

Lussinge and I would often go there. In the evening we would meet, on the boulevard, M. Darbelles, a man six feet tall, our childhood friend, but a real bore. He would tell us about Court de Gébelin and he wanted to advance his career through science. He has been more fortunate by other means, as he is a minister today. He would go to see his mother in the rue Caumartin; to get rid of him, we would go into Maisonnette's house.

That summer, I started to come back to life a little and take an interest in the ideas of this world. I managed to stop thinking of Milan for five or six hours at a time; only waking up was still a bitter experience for me. Sometimes I would stay in my bed until midday, brooding. So I would listen to the description, in M[aisonne]tte's mouth, of the way *power*, the only real thing, was distributed in Paris in those days, in 1821.

On arriving in a town I always ask:

1. which are the twelve prettiest women;
2. which are the twelve richest men;
3. which is the man who could get me hanged.

M[aisonne]tte answered my questions quite well. The surprising thing for me was that his love for the word *King* was in good faith. 'What a word for a Frenchman!' he would say to me enthusiastically, his dark little eyes darting here and there and looking up heavenwards, 'what a word: *the King!*' Maisonnette was a teacher in the class of rhetoric in 1811, he spontaneously gave his pupils the day off to celebrate the birth of the King of Rome. In 1815, he wrote a pamphlet in favour of the Bourbons. M. Decazes read it, summoned him and made him a political writer with a salary of eight thousand francs. Today, M[aisonne]tte is a convenient person for a prime minister: he knows with perfect certainty, like a dictionary, all the little facts, all the inside stories of the political intrigues in Paris from 1815 to 1832.

I failed to see this merit, which only becomes evident when you ask the right questions. All I was aware of was this incredible way of reasoning.

I would say to myself, 'Who is being mocked here? Is it me? But to what purpose? Is it Lussinge? Is it that poor young man in a grey frock-coat, who's so ugly with his snub nose?' That young man had something brazen and extremely displeasing about him. His little lacklustre eyes always had the same expression and this expression was malicious.

This was my first view of the best of my current friends. I'm not too sure about his inner feelings, but I am sure about his talents: he's Count Gazul, today so well known, and when I received a letter from him last week, it made me happy for two days.* He must have been eighteen years old, having been born, I seem to remember, in 1804. I could easily believe, with Buffon, that we take a great deal after our mothers, all jokes on the uncertainty of our fatherhood apart – an uncertainty which is very rare for the first child.

This theory seems to me to be confirmed by Count Gazul. His mother has a great deal of French wit and a superior reason. Like her son, she seems susceptible to the sway of tender feelings once a year. I find a sensation of *dryness* in several of M. Gazul's works, but I have great hopes for the future.

At the time of the pretty little garden in the rue Caumartin, Gazul was in his rhetoric class, with the most abominable master. The word abominable is quite astonished to find itself coupled to the name of Maisonnette, the best of men. But such was his taste in the arts: he liked things that were false, brilliant, vaudevillian above all.

He was the pupil of M. Luce de Lancival whom I met in my early youth at the home of M. de Maisonnette**, who didn't have his plays published, even though they had *met with success*. This fine fellow did

---

* *Made*[77] 14 pages on 2nd July from five to seven. I wouldn't have been able to work like this on a work of the imagination like *The Red and the Black*.
Edwards.
** 3rd July [1832].

me the great service of saying that I had a superior wit. 'You mean a *superior pride*,' said Martial Daru, with a laugh: he thought I was almost stupid. But I forgave him for everything: he would take me to see Clotilde (who was at the time the first dancer in the Opera). Sometimes – what days there were for me! – I would find myself in his box at the Opera and in front of me, fourth, she would dress and undress. What a moment for a provincial lad!

Luce de Lancival had a wooden leg and a great degree of kindness; moreover, he would have slipped a pun into a tragedy. I imagine that this is what Dorat must have thought on artistic matters. I've found the right turn of phrase: he's a shepherd from Boucher. Perhaps in 1860 there will still be paintings by Boucher in the Museum.

Maisonnette had been Luce's pupil, and Gazul is Maisonnette's. In the same way, Annibale Carracci is the pupil of the Flemish painter Calvart[78].

Over and above his passion, as prodigious as it was sincere, for the reigning minister, and his bravery, Maisonnette had another quality that I like: he earned twenty-two thousand francs from the minister to prove to the French that the Bourbons were adorable, and he squandered thirty.

Having sometimes written for twelve hours at a stretch to persuade the French, M[aisonne]tte would go to see an honest woman of the people to whom he offered five hundred francs. He was ugly, short, but he had such a Spanish fire that after three visits those ladies would forget his bizarre face and see only the sublimity of the five-hundred-franc banknote.

I have to add something for the eyes of an honest and well-behaved woman, if ever such eyes come to rest on these pages. Firstly, five hundred francs in 1822 is the equivalent of one thousand in 1872. Then, a charming ticket-seller admitted that before Maisonnette's five-hundred-franc banknote, she had never had a double napoleon to call her own. Rich people are perfectly unjust and perfectly comic when they set themselves up as the disdainful judges of all the sins and crimes committed for money. Look at the terrible fawning, and the ten years of petty kowtowing they impose on themselves at Court to obtain a portfolio. Look at the life of Duke Decazes after his fall from power in

1820, after Louvel's action, until now.

So here I am, in 1822, spending three evenings a week at the opera buffa and one or two at the home of Maisonnette, in the rue Caumartin. When I've been feeling low, evenings have always been the most difficult period in my daily life. On opera days, from midnight to two o'clock, I was at the home of Mme Pasta with Lussinge, Missirini, Fiori, etc.

I almost fought a duel with a very cheery and very fine fellow who wanted me to introduce him at Mme Pasta's. This was the amiable Edward Edwards, that Englishman, the only one of his race who habitually spread gaiety around him, my travelling companion on my trip to England, the man who in London wanted to fight a duel on my behalf.

You haven't forgotten that he had warned me of a nasty mistake: not having paid enough attention to an offensive insinuation made by a mere peasant, the captain of a boat in Calais.

I declined to introduce him. It was evening, and this poor Edwards, at 9 p.m., was no longer the same man he was in the morning.

'Do you know, my dear B***,' he said to me, 'that it would be well within my rights to feel offended?'

'Do you know, my dear Edwards, that I have as much pride as you and that I am perfectly indifferent to your vexation, etc., etc.?'

This all went quite far. I can shoot very well, I hit nine dolls out of twelve. (M. Prosper Mérimée has seen me do so at the Luxembourg shooting-stall.)* Edwards could also shoot well, perhaps not quite so well as me.

Anyway, this quarrel increased our friendship. I remember it because, with a muddle-headedness quite characteristic of me, I asked him, the next day or the day after that at the latest, to introduce me to the famous Dr Edwards his brother, who was the talk of the town in 1822. He killed a thousand frogs a month and was rumoured to be about to discover how we breathe and a cure for the chest diseases of pretty women. You know that, every year in Paris, the cold kills 1,100 young women as they leave the ball. I've seen the official figures.

Now, the knowledgeable, wise, calm, hard-working Dr Edwards had

* 3rd July [1832].

but little time for the friends of his brother Edward. To begin with, the doctor had sixteen brothers and my friend was the biggest scoundrel of the lot. It was because of his excessively cheery tone and his passionate love of the worst possible jokes that he could not let go by if they sprang to his mind, that I'd been unwilling to take him to Mme Pasta's. He had a big head, the handsome eyes of a drunkard, and the nattiest blond hair I've ever seen. Without this infernal mania for trying to be as witty as a Frenchman, he would have been really nice, and he could have had every chance of the most resounding success with women, as I will mention when I talk about *Eugeny*, but she is still so young that perhaps it's wrong to talk about her in these ramblings which may be published ten years after my death. If I put twenty, all the *nuances of life* will have changed, the reader will only see the broad sweeps. And what the hell is the point of *broad sweeps* when it comes to these games I play with my pen? This is something to be examined.

I think [that] to avenge himself nobly – for he had a noble soul when it wasn't clouded by fifty glasses of aquavit – Edwards worked hard to obtain permission to introduce me to the doctor.

It was a little, arch-bourgeois salon; a woman of the greatest merit who talked morality and whom I took to be a *quakeress* and finally in the shape of the doctor a man of the rarest merit hidden in a puny little body from which life seemed to be leaking away. You couldn't see it in this salon (rue du Helder, No. 12). I was given a cold reception.

What a damn silly idea: getting myself introduced to them! It was an unforeseeable whim, quite mad. Basically, if there was anything I wanted, it was to get to know people. Every month perhaps this idea came back to me, but the tastes, the passions, the hundred follies that filled my life, had to leave the surface of the water calm for this image to appear. Then I would say to myself, 'I'm not like ***, like ***,' fatuous men I was acquainted with. I don't choose my friends.

I pick up at random what destiny places in my path.

This phrase has been my source of pride for ten years.

I needed three years of diligent attentiveness to overcome the repugnance and alarm that I inspired in Mme Edwards' salon. They viewed me as a Don Juan (see Mozart and Molière), as a monster of seduction and diabolical wit. Certainly it wouldn't have cost me any more to be tolerated in the salon of Mme de Talaru, or Mme de Duras, or Mme de Broglie who regularly allowed middle-class people in, or that of Mme Guizot whom I liked (I mean Mlle Pauline de Meulan), or even in Mme Récamier's salon.

But, in 1822, I hadn't understood the full importance of the answer to this question asked about any man who publishes a book that gets read:

'*What kind of man is he?*'

I was saved from scorn by this answer: 'He often goes to the salon of Mme de Tracy.' The society of 1829 needs to scorn the man in whose books, rightly or wrongly, it discovers a certain wit. It is afraid, it is no longer an impartial judge. How would it have been if people had answered: 'He often goes to the salon of Mme de Duras (Mlle de Kersaint)'?

Well, even today, when I know the importance of these answers, and because of this very importance, I would abandon the fashionable salon. (I've just deserted the salon of *Lady Holye* – in 1832.)

I remained faithful to the salon of Dr Edwards, who wasn't likeable, as one is faithful to an ugly mistress, because I could leave it every Wednesday (this was Mme Edwards' day).

I will submit to everything through the caprice of the moment; if one day I am told, 'Tomorrow you will have to submit to this or that moment of boredom,' my imagination turns it into a monster, and I'd rather throw myself out of the window than be taken to a boring salon.

At the home of Mme Edwards, I got to know M. Stritch, an impassive and gloomy Englishman, perfectly decent, a victim of the aristocracy, for he was an Irishman and a solicitor, and yet defended, as essential to his honour, the prejudices sown and cultivated in English heads by the aristocracy. I have rediscovered this strange absurdity mixed with the greatest decency and the most perfect delicacy in M. Rogers, near Birmingham (at whose home I spent some time in August 1826). This kind of personality is very common in England. For the ideas sown and cultivated through the interest of the aristocracy, one might say – and it's saying a great deal – that the Englishman lacks logic nearly as much as a German.

The Englishman's sense of logic, so admirable in finance and in everything associated with an art that brings in money at the end of each week, becomes confused and loses its thread as soon as you rise to somewhat more abstract subjects that *don't directly bring in any money*. They have become idiotic in discussions relating to refined literature through the same mechanism which leads idiots to the service of the diplomacy *of the King of French*[79]; you can choose from only a very small number of men. Such-and-such a man, made to discuss the genius of Shakespeare and Cervantes (great men who died the same day, 16th April 16**, I believe), is a cotton merchant in Manchester. He would reproach himself with wasting his time if he were to open a book not directly related to cotton and its export to Germany when it is spun, etc., etc.

In the same way the *k[in]g of Fr[ench]*[80] chooses his diplomats only from among young men of high birth or great fortune. You have to look for talent in the place where M. Thiers was brought up (he sold himself in 1830). He's the son of a petty bourgeois from Aix-en-Provence.

Having reached the summer of 1822, more or less a year after my departure from Milan, I now only rarely thought of slipping voluntarily out of this world. My life was gradually filling up, not with pleasant things, but all the same with ordinary things that came between myself and the last happiness which had comprised the object of my worship.

I had two perfectly innocent pleasures:

1. to chat after dinner while going [for] a walk with Lussinge or some man of my acquaintance; I had eight or ten such; all of them, as usual, presented to me by chance;

2. when it was warm, going to read the English papers in Galignani's garden. There I reread with delight four or five novels by Walter Scott. The first, the one with Henry Morton and Sergeant Boswell (*Old Mortality*, I think) brought back to mind my vivid memories of Volterra. I'd often opened it by chance, while waiting for Métilde in Florence, in Molini's literary cabinet on the Arno. I read it as a memory of 1818.

I had long quarrels with Lussinge. I maintained that a good third of Sir Walter Scott's merit was due to a secretary who sketched out descriptions of the countryside for him, in the presence of nature. I found him, as I still do, lacking in force when it comes to depicting passion, and in his knowledge of the human heart. Will posterity confirm the judgement of contemporaries, which places the arch-conservative baronet immediately below Shakespeare?

But I detest him as a person and I have refused several times to see him (in Paris, through M. de Mirbel, in Naples in 1832, in Rome, *idem*). Fox gave him a job with a salary of fifty or a hundred thousand francs and he used it to slander adroitly Lord Byron who took advantage of this lesson in the higher hypocrisy: see the letter Lord Byron wrote to me in 1823.[81]

Have you ever seen, gentle reader,* a silkworm that has eaten enough mulberry leaf? The comparison isn't very dignified, but it is so apposite! This ugly beast doesn't want to eat any more, it needs to climb up and spin its silk prison.

Such is the animal known as a 'writer'. For anyone who has enjoyed the profound occupation of writing, reading is merely a secondary pleasure. So often I thought it was two o'clock; I looked at my clock: it was half-past six. This is my only excuse for having blackened so much paper.

As moral health returned to me in the summer of 1822, I thought of publishing a book entitled *On Love*, pencilled in Milan on my walks as I thought about Métilde. I intended to rewrite it in Paris and it really needs it. To think with any depth of those sorts of things made me too sad. It meant roughly handling a wound that had hardly healed over. I transcribed in ink what was still in pencil.

My friend Edwards found a bookseller for me (M. Mongie) who gave me nothing for my manuscript and promised me half the profits, if there ever were any.

Today, now that chance has enabled me to earn my stripes, I receive letters from booksellers quite unknown to me (1832, June, from M. Thierry, I think) who offer to pay me in ready money for my manuscripts. I had no idea of this whole mechanism of base literature. It filled me with horror and might even have put me entirely off writing. The scheming of M. Hugo (see *Gazette des Tribunaux* in 1831, I think, his lawsuit with the bookseller Bossan[ge] or Plassan), the manoeuvres of M. de Chateaubriand, the errands run by Béranger, but they are

* 3rd July 1832.

justifiable. That great poet had been deprived by the Bourbons of his job with a salary of 1,800 francs in the Ministry of the Interior.

'*Re schiocchi, re ***'*[82]

Three lines by Monti.

The stupidity of the B[ourbons] appears in all its obviousness. If they hadn't basely deprived this poor clerk of his job for a song that was light-hearted rather than malicious, that great poet wouldn't have cultivated his talent and would never have become one of the most powerful levers that prised the Bourbons out of office. He light-heartedly formulated the contempt felt by the French for that *Rotten Throne*. This is what the Queen of Spain called them, the one who died in Rome and was the friend of the Prince of Peace.

By chance, I got to know this Court, but writing anything other than an analysis of the human heart bores me. If chance had given me a secretary, I would have been a different kind of author. – We have quite enough of *this* kind, says the devil's advocate.

That old queen had brought from Spain to Rome an old confessor. This confessor was keeping the daughter-in-law of the *chef* of the French Academy. This Spaniard, a very old man but still with an eye for the ladies, had the imprudence to say (here I can't give the amusing details, the mummers are still alive), anyway, to say that Ferdinand VII was the son of so-and-so, and not of Charles IV, this was one of the great sins of the old queen. She had died. A spy found out what the priest had said. Ferdinand had him kidnapped in Rome and yet, instead of having him poisoned, some counter-intrigue I am ignorant of had this old man thrown into the *Presides*[83].

Dare I say which illness this old queen full of common sense was suffering from? (I found out in Rome in 1817 or 1824.) It was a series of love affairs that had left behind an illness that failed to clear up, so that she couldn't fall without breaking a bone. The poor woman, being a queen, was ashamed of these frequent accidents and didn't dare have herself treated properly. I found the same kind of misfortune at the Court of Napoleon in 1811. I was well-acquainted, alas! with the excellent Cullerier (the uncle, the father, in a word Cullerier the elder; the younger strikes me as a conceited person)[84]. I brought three ladies to him: I blindfolded two of them (rue de l'Odéon, No. 26).

He told me two days later that they had been feverish (an effect of modesty and not of disease). This perfectly gallant man never lifted his eyes to look at them.

It's always fortunate for the race of the Bourbons to be rid of a monster like Ferdinand VII. The Duke de Laval, a perfectly decent man but a nobleman and a duke (which constitutes two mental illnesses), did himself honour in telling me about Ferdinand VII's friendship. And yet he had been an ambassador at his Court for three years.

This recalls the deep hatred felt by Louis XVI for Franklin. That prince found a really Bourbonesque means of avenging himself: he had the face of the venerable old man painted at the bottom of a porcelain chamber-pot.

Mme Campan told us this at the home of Mme Cardon (rue de Lille, at the corner of the rue de Bellechasse), after the 18th Brumaire. The memoirs of the time that were read at Mme Cardon's were poles apart from the sentimental rhapsody that brings tears to the eyes of the most distinguished women of the *Faubourg* Saint-Honoré (which led to one of them being stripped of their glamour in my feeble eyes, around 1827).

CHAPTER TEN

So here I was with something to keep me busy during the summer of 1822. Correcting the proofs of *On Love* printed in duodecimo, on poor-quality paper. M. Mongie swore to me indignantly that he had been cheated over the quality of the paper. I didn't know what booksellers were like in 1822. I'd only ever done business with M. Pierre Didot, whom I paid for all the paper as in accordance with his tariff. M. Mongie had a good laugh at my idiotic naivety. 'Ah, this fellow just *doesn't have his head screwed on the right way!*', he would say, guffawing as he compared me to other authors in the trade such as Ancelot, or Vitet, or *** Well, I later found out that M. Mongie was far and away the most honest of booksellers. What can I say about my friend, M. Sautelet, a young solicitor, my friend before he became a bookseller?

But the poor devil killed himself for sorrow on seeing himself abandoned by a rich widow called Mme Bonnet or Bourdet, some noble name of the kind who gave her preference to a young peer of the realm (these words were starting to sound quite seductive in 1828). This happy peer was, I think,[*] M. Pérignon, who'd had my friend Mme Viganò, the daughter of the great man (in 1820, I think).

It was a thoroughly dangerous thing for me to be correcting the proofs of a book that reminded me, in all their diverse shades, of so many of the emotions I had felt in Italy. I succumbed to the temptation of taking a room in Montmorency. I would go there in the evening, a two-hour journey with the coach from the rue Saint-Denis. In the midst of the woods, especially to the left of the Sablonnière where the road rises, I would correct my proofs. I almost went mad.

The crazy ideas of returning to Milan that I had so often repressed kept returning with surprising force. I don't know how I managed to resist. The force of passion, which means you have only one thing in your head, takes away every memory, at the distance I am now from those times. All I can distinctly remember is the shape of the trees of that part of the woods in Montmorency.

What is called the valley of M[ontmorency] is merely a promontory

[*] 3rd July [18]32.

94

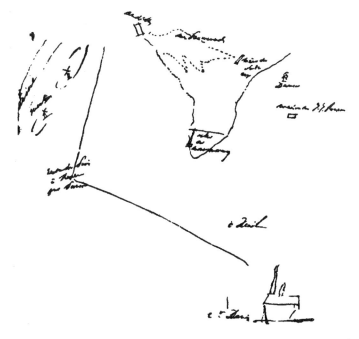

Paris

jutting out towards the valley of the Seine and directly over the dome of the Invalides.*

When Lanfranc painted** a dome 150 feet high, he would exaggerate certain characteristics. '*L'aria dipinge* (the air takes over the job of painting),' he would say. Likewise, as people will be much less duped by *Kings*[85], nobles and priests round 1870 than they are today, I'm tempted by the idea of exaggerating certain characteristics against those vermin of the human race. But I resist: it would mean being *false to truth,*

False to his bed…

Cymbeline.

* 3rd July, tired after 26 pages.
** 3rd July, 27 pages.

But – why don't I have a secretary so I can dictate facts, anecdotes and not abstract discussions about these three things? But having written twenty-seven pages today, I'm too tired to enumerate in detail the anecdotes that I'm sure of, that I saw, and that are laying siege to my memory.

CHAPTER ELEVEN

I would go quite often to correct the proofs of *On Love* in the grounds of Mme Doligny's country house at Corbeil. There I could avoid falling into sad reveries; hardly had I completed my work than I would return to the salon.

I came really close to finding happiness in 1824. Thinking of France during the six or seven years that I spent in Milan, hoping fervently that I would never return to a Paris sullied by the Bourbons, or indeed France, I said to myself, 'A single woman would have made me forgive that country, Countess Fanny Berthois.' I loved her in 1824. We had been thinking of each other ever since I'd seen her with bare feet in 1814, the day after the Battle of Montmirail or Champaubert, entering at 6 a.m. the home of her mother, the M*** of N., to ask for news of how it had turned out. Well, Mme Berthois was in the countryside at the home of her friend, Mme Doligny. When I finally resolved to exhibit my gloom at Mme Doligny's, she said to me, 'Mme Berthois has been waiting for you. She left me only the day before yesterday because something terrible has happened: she has just lost one of her charming daughters.'

Coming from the lips of a woman as sensible as Mme Doligny, these words had considerable import. In 1814, she had said to me, 'Mme Berthois takes you at your full worth.' In 1823 or [18]22, Mme Berthois had the kindness to love me a little. Mme Doligny said to her one day, 'Your eyes keep resting on Belle; if he had a taller, slimmer figure, he'd have long since told you that he loves you.'

This wasn't quite true. My melancholy gazed with pleasure on Mme Berthois' eyes, so beautiful. In my stupidity, I didn't take it any further. I didn't say to myself, 'Why is that young woman looking at me?' I altogether forgot the excellent lessons in love that I had been given once upon a time by my uncle Gagnon and my friend and protector Martial Daru. My uncle Gagnon, born in Grenoble around 1765, really was a charming man. His conversation, which struck men as being like a grandiloquent and elegant novel, struck women as being delightful. He was always droll, delicate, full of those turns of phrase that can mean anything if you let them. He had none of that gaiety that intimidates people, as has become my lot. It was difficult to be more attractive and less reasonable than my uncle Gagnon. Thus he didn't capitalise on his fortune with others. Young men envied him without being able to imitate him. *Mature* men, as they say in Grenoble, found him *superficial*. This word is quite enough to kill off anyone's reputation. My uncle, although a thorough ultra, like my whole family in 1815, having even emigrated round 1792, was never able under Louis XVIII to be a councillor at the Royal Court of Grenoble; and this at a time when they were filling this Court with rascals such as Faure, the notary, etc., etc., and with people who boasted that they had never read the abominable Civil Code of the Revolution. On the other hand, my uncle had precisely all the pretty women who around 1788 made Grenoble into one of the most agreeable of provincial towns. The famous Laclos whom I knew, an old artillery general, in the staff box at Milan, and to whom I paid court because of *Dangerous Liaisons*, learning from me that I came from Grenoble, *was really touched*.

My uncle*, then, when he saw me leaving for the *Ecole polytechnique* in November 1799, took me to one side to give me two louis that I refused, which doubtless pleased him, for he had two or three apartments in town, and not much money. After which, taking on a paternal air which greatly touched me, as he had admirable eyes, those big eyes which tend to squint at the least emotion, he said to me:

'My friend, you think you're a bright lad, you are full of an un-bearable pride because of your successes in the mathematics schools, but none of this is of any importance. It is possible to make progress in the world only through women. Now, you're ugly, but people will never reproach you with your ugliness, as you have an interesting physiognomy. Your mistresses will leave you; but just remember this: when one is in the process of being left, there's nothing easier than to look ridiculous. After which, a man is good for nothing except to be thrown to the dogs in the eyes of the other local women. In the twenty-four hours after she has left you, make a declaration to another woman; and if you can't do any better, make a declaration to a chambermaid.'

Whereupon, he embraced me and I climbed into the mail-coach for Lyon. Happy if I had remembered the advice of that master

* 21st June [1832].

tactician! How many successes I've missed! How many humiliations I've suffered! But if I had been more astute, I'd have become disgusted to the point of nausea with women, and thus with music and painting like my two contemporaries. MM. de la [Ro]sière and [Per]rochin. They are desiccated, disgusted with the world, philosophers. Instead of that, in everything concerning women, I have the good fortune to be as naive as at the age of twenty-five.

This is the reason why I will never blow out my brains in disgust at everything, out of boredom with life. In the career of literature I still see a host of things to be done. I have enough potential works to write to keep myself busy for ten lives. The difficulty, right now, 1832, is to get used to not being distracted by the action of drawing a bill for twenty thousand francs from the head cashier for central expenditure of the Paris Treasury.

CHAPTER TWELVE

I don't know* who took me to M. de l'Etang's. Someone had given him, if I remember, a copy of the *History of Painting in Italy*, on the pretext of a review in the *Lycée*, one of those ephemeral papers created in Paris by the success of the *Edinburgh Review*. He wished to make my acquaintance.

In England, the aristocracy despises literature. In Paris, literature occupies too important a position. It's impossible for French people living in Paris to tell the truth about the works of other French people living in Paris. I have made eight or ten deadly enemies for having told the editors of the *Globe*, in the guise of good advice and speaking directly to them, that the *Globe* had a rather too puritanical tone and perhaps wasn't sufficiently *witty*.

A conscientious literary journal as the *Edinburgh Review* once was, is possible for only as long as it is printed in Geneva, and run from there by a man with a good commercial brain capable of keeping a secret. The director should make a yearly trip to Paris, and receive in Geneva the articles for that month's journal. He should choose, pay well (two hundred francs per printed page) and should never name his editors.

So I was taken to M. de l'Etang's one Sunday at two o'clock. It was at this inconvenient time that he would receive visitors. You had to climb up ninety-five steps, as he held his academy on the sixth floor of a house that belonged to him and his sisters, in the rue Gaillon. From his little windows all you could see was a forest of chimneys in blackish plaster. For me, this is one of the ugliest views, but the four little rooms in which M. de l'Etang lived were embellished with engravings and curious and agreeable *objets d'art*.

There was a superb portrait of Cardinal Richelieu that I would often look at. Next to it was the flabby, heavy, ponderous, inane face of Racine. It was long before growing so fat that this great poet had experienced the emotions whose memory was indispensable to write *Andromaque* and *Phèdre*.

At M. de l'Etang's, I met, in front of a paltry little fire, as it was, if I remember, in February 1822 that I was taken there, eight or ten people

* 4th July 1832, Mme Malibran.

who were talking about everything. I was struck by their good sense, their wit, and above all by the fine tact of the master of the house who, with the greatest discretion, would direct the discussion in such a way that people never spoke three at a time and never relapsed into morose moments of silence.

I cannot speak too highly of this circle. I have never encountered anything, I won't say superior, but even comparable to it. I was struck on the first day and, twenty times perhaps during the three or four years it lasted, I surprised myself performing the same act of admiration.

Such a circle is possible only in the country of Voltaire, Molière, and Courier.

It is impossible in England, for at M. de l'Etang's they would have made as much fun of a duke as of anyone else – more than of anyone else if he'd been ridiculous.

Germany couldn't produce it: there they are too used to believing enthusiastically in the fashionable inanities of philosophy (M. Ancillon's angels). In any case, outside their enthusiasm, the Germans are too stupid.

The Italians would have held forth, everyone would have taken the floor for twenty minutes and would have remained the deadly enemy of his antagonist in the discussion. At the third session, they'd have written satirical sonnets against each other.

For here, the discussion was firm and frank, on everything and with everyone. They were polite at M. de l'Etang's, but because of him. It was often necessary for him to cover the retreat of the imprudent spirits who, trying to come up with a new idea, had put forward something all too obviously absurd.

There I met M. de l'Etang, MM. Albert Stapfer, J.-J. Ampère, Sautelet, de Lussinge…

M. de l'Etang is a character* in the mould of the good Vicar of Wakefield. To give an idea of him you would need all the half-tones of Goldsmith or Addison.

Firstly, he's extremely ugly; above all he has – as is rare in Paris – a low, plebeian forehead, he is well proportioned and quite tall.

* 4th July 1832. First hot weather.

He has all the pettiness of a bourgeois. If he buys for thirty-six francs a dozen handkerchiefs at the corner s[ho]p, two hours later he thinks that his handkerchiefs are a rarity, and that you could not find similar ones for love nor money in Paris.*

* The heat is stopping me having ideas at half-past one.

1. 'Mero' is Rome.

2. Métilde (Mathilde Viscontini, wife of Jan Dembowski) was the love of Stendhal's life.

3. In fact, this is an allusion to Marivaux.

4. 'The c***' is, of course, the clap.

5. The last two works, humanistic and classical in tone, are by the Abbé Barthélemy (1716–95) and Charles Rollin (1661–1741) respectively. Diderot was a writer much closer to Stendhal's experimentalist aesthetic.

6. Perhaps: 'to kill Louis XVIII'.

7. The *Roman comique* (published 1651 and 1657), by Paul Scarron (1610–60), a novel about play-actors; La Rancune ('Rancour') is a character in it.

8. 15th September 1826 was the date on which Stendhal separated from his mistress, Clémentine Curial.

9. Vittorio Alfieri (1749–1803) was an Italian poet and dramatist.

10. Georges Cuvier (1769–1832), the famous comparative anatomist.

11. Written in English.

12. Stendhal is here referring to the military conspiracy of 19th August 1820.

13. Louvel assassinated the Duke de Berry (13th June 1820).

14. Written in English.

15. 'Belle' is a nickname for 'Beyle', as in Henri Beyle, Stendhal's 'real' name.

16. A quotation from Racine's *Britannicus* (1669).

17. Babilano Pallavicini was a seventeenth-century Genoese nobleman, who was taken to court by his wife on a charge of impotence.

18. Destutt de Tracy (1754–1836), one of the leading 'Idéologues', a school of materialist and sensualist philosophers inspired by Condillac.

19. Marie-Joseph Paul Yves Roch Gilbert Motier, Marquis de La Fayette (1757–1834). Despite his democratic inclinations, La Fayette remained loyal to the French royal family, and in 1830 he helped to bring Louis-Philippe to power.

20. The Count de Provence is reported to have said, 'Phew! Let's go and eat,' on learning that his accomplice, the Marquis de Favras, had been hanged without betraying his (the Count's) own part in the foiled plot.

21. Dangeau was a memorialist at the Court of Louis XIV.

22. The Count de Ségur claimed that he asked the English ambassador for his pen so that he could send a note aimed against English interests.

23. Written in English.

24. Written in English.

25. The date of the July Revolution which put Louis-Philippe on the throne.

26. *Mezzo termine*: a halfway house (Italian).

27. Institute: the Institut de France, the body of learned societies that includes the French Academy. M. D. refers to Etienne-Jean Delécluze (1781–1863; Stendhal here misspells his name), the painter and art critic.

28. Angelica's ring, in Ariosto's Renaissance epic *Orlando Furioso* (1532), made her invisible – a frequent fantasy of Stendhal.

29. The German philosopher was, according to Stendhal's editors, Philippe-Jacob Müller.

30. Epaminondas was a great Theban general of the fourth century BC.

31. Lord Brougham (1778–1868) was a lawyer and man of letters; Vincenzo Monti (1754–1828) was an Italian poet and patriot, Antonio Canova (1757–1822) was an Italian sculptor; and Gioacchino Rossini (1792–1868) an Italian operatic composer.

32. 'Ultraliberals' were extremist supporters of the Republic – the opposite of 'ultras', the ultramonarchists.

33. Augustin Thierry (1795–1856) was a French historian; his brother, Amédée (1797–1873), was also a historian.

34. Pierre-Jean-Georges Cabanis (1757–1808), an Idéologue like de Tracy, and a physician and materialist philosopher.

35. A reference to Voltaire's *L'Ingénu* (1767): the Huron is an energetic outsider.

36. Stendhal's love of the music of Domenico Cimarosa (1749–1801) dated back to the first time he heard Cimerosa's opera *Il Matrimonio segreto* (1792), which he occasionally rated more highly than Mozart.

37. Faro is a card-game that was popular in the eighteenth and nineteenth centuries.

38. Written in English.

39. Garde des Sceaux: the French Minister of Justice, the approximate equivalent of the British Lord Chancellor.

40. 'Dominique' was one of Stendhal's names for himself.

41. 'Don't think about it!' (Italian).

42. The inscription on this imaginary tombstone reads: Errico Beyle, Milanese; lived, wrote, loved; this soul adored Cimarosa, Mozart and Shakespeare; he died at the age of ** on the *** 18**

43. 'Here you will breathe the dark freshness': a slight misquotation from Virgil, *Eclogues*, I, 52–3.

44. Stendhal adds a 'phonetic' transcription of the actor's name for French readers ('Kîne').

45. *Jupiter Mansuetus*: a statue that for Stendhal encapsulated the sculptor's capacity to create 'character' more effectively than painting.

46. Henri Brulard was one of Stendhal's pseudonyms.

47. Oliver Goldsmith's *She Stoops to Conquer* (1773) and Pierre Marivaux's *The Game of Life and Chance* (1730) are remarkably similar in plot.

48. The *Memoirs of the Life of Colonel Hutchinson* (published 1806) were written by the wife of one of Cromwell's lieutenants.

49. *The Indian Cottage* is a work by Bernardin de Saint-Pierre (1737–1814).

50. John Cam Hobhouse (1786–1869) was a friend of Byron.

51. The Congrégation: a former religious society, associated in Stendhal's time with the ultras.

52. The *Faubourg* Saint-Germain: the area on the left bank of the Seine inhabited by many of the great noble families of France.

53. Germinal VIII: the month Germinal (March/April) of the revolutionary year VIII (1800).

54. Written in English.

55. Written in English.

56. J.-B. Say (1767–1832) and Adam Smith (1723–90) were both famous economists.

57. Mme Périer was Stendhal's much-loved sister Pauline. He remained very fond of her, even though she eventually became a liability to his bachelor existence.

58. Written in English.

59. Written in English.

60. The Carbonari were a mainly Italian revolutionary society.

61. Stendhal is here perhaps approximating to the Italian '*scolazione*', gonorrhoea.

62. Written in English.

63. Missirini was the name used by Stendhal for Alexandre Micheroux.

64. Boileau, *Epître* IX, 60.

65. From Voltaire's play *Zaïre* (1732).

66. Written in English.

67. This was the date of Napoleon's seizure of power.

68. Some editors have deduced from a 'ti' in the manuscript that the missing word is 'tyranny'.

69. Franz Joseph Gall (1758–1828) was a celebrated phrenologist.

70. Written in English.

71. Gazul: Stendhal's name for Mérimée (1803–70), best known for his story 'Carmen' (1845) but also the author of *Le théâtre de Clara Gazul* (1825).

72. Themistocles claimed that the laurels of Miltiades, the victor of Marathon (and thus his own rival), kept him awake at night.

73. *La Minerve* was, unlike the *Journal des Débats*, a liberal newspaper.

74. The Abbé Cotin was mocked by Boileau; *amareggiata* means embittered (Italian).

75. Victorine was a fashionable dressmaker.

76. All these songs are by Pierre Jean de Béranger (1780–1857), a republican poet whose songs helped inspire the revolutionaries in 1830.

77. Written in English.

78. Denis Calvert (or Calvaert) (1540–1619) was born in Flanders but co-founded the Bolognese school of painting.

79. Written in English.

80. Written in English.

81. The letter Stendhal refers to was sent on 29th May 1823. Stendhal replied on 23rd June. Byron's original letter was published the following year.

82. 'Stupid kings, *** kings' (Italian).

83. *Presides*: a place of deportation on the coast of Africa.

84. Michel Cullerier (1758–1827), a doctor specialising in venereal diseases.

85. Written in English.

The Privileges

God[1] gives me the following warrant:

Article 1

Never any serious illness until a ripe old age: and then, no pain, but death, by apoplexy, in bed while asleep without any pain either spiritual or physical. Every year, no more than three days of illness. The corpus, and what comes out of it, odourless.

Article 2

The following miracles will be neither noticed nor suspected by anyone.

Article 3

The *mentula*[2], like the index finger, for hardness and for movement; this whenever desired. The shape two inches more than the toe [?], same breadth. But pleasure through the *mentula* only twice a week. Twenty times a year the beneficiary will be able to change into any person he wishes, provided this person exists. A hundred times a year he will know for twenty-four hours any language he wishes.

Article 3 [= 4]

Miracle. The beneficiary, when wearing a ring on his finger and squeezing this ring while looking at a woman, will make her fall in love with him, passionately, as we think Héloise to have been in love with Abélard. If the ring is moistened with a little saliva, the woman he is looking at merely becomes a tender and devoted friend. Looking at a woman and taking off a ring from the finger, the feelings inspired by virtue of the preceding privileges cease. Hatred changes into benevolence when looking at the hateful person and rubbing a ring on the finger. These miracles can take place only four times a year for passionate love, eight times for friendship, twenty times for the cessation of hatred, and fifty times for the inspiring of simple benevolence.

Article 4 [= 5]

Fine hair, excellent teeth, fine skin never grazed. A sweet, light odour. On the 1st of February and the 1st of June of every year, the beneficiary's clothes become as they were on the third time he wore them.

Article 5 [= 6]

Miracles. In the eyes of all those who don't know me, the beneficiary will have the appearance of General de Belle who died at San Domingo, but with no imperfection.[3] He will play perfectly well whist, écarté, billiards, chess, but will never be able to win more than a hundred francs; he will go pistol-shooting, horse-riding, and duelling, all to perfection.

Article 6 [= 7]

Miracle. Four times a year he will be able to change into whichever animal he wants, and then change back into a man. Four times a year he will be able to change into whichever man he wants, and also concentrate his life in that of an animal which, in the case of the death or hindrance of man No. 1 into which he has changed, will be able to restore him to the natural shape of the beneficiary. Thus the beneficiary will be able four times a year and for an unlimited time on each occasion to occupy two bodies at once.

Article 7 [= 8]

When the man given these privileges wears on himself or on his finger for two minutes a ring he has placed for a few seconds in his mouth, he will become invulnerable for the time he has designated. He will have the sight of an eagle ten times a year and will be able to run five leagues in an hour.

Article 8 [= 9]

Every day at two o'clock in the morning the beneficiary will find in his pocket a gold napoleon, plus the value of forty francs in the current legal tender of the country he happens to be in. The sums that have been stolen from him will be found the following night, at two o'clock in the morning, on a table before him. Assassins, at the moment they strike him, or administer poison to him, will have an acute attack of cholera lasting a week. The beneficiary will be able to shorten these pains by saying, 'I pray that the sufferings of so-and-so cease, or are changed into some lesser pain.' Thieves will be afflicted by an acute attack of cholera, lasting two days, at the time they start to commit the theft.

Article 10

When hunting, eight times a year, a little flag will indicate to the beneficiary, at a distance of one league, the game to be found there and its exact position. One second before the game animal heads off, the little flag will glow; naturally, this little flag will be invisible to anyone other than the beneficiary.

Article 11

A similar flag will indicate to the beneficiary the statues hidden in the earth, in rivers and streams and behind walls; what these statues are, when and by whom they were made and the price they might fetch once they have been discovered. The beneficiary will be able to change these statues into a ball of lead weighing a quarter of an ounce. This miracle of the flag and the successive changing into a ball and into a statue can take place only eight times a year.

Article 12

The animal ridden by the beneficiary, or pulling the vehicle carrying him, will never be ill, and will never fall down. The beneficiary will be able to unite with this animal so as to inspire it with his wishes and to share its sensations. Thus, the beneficiary when riding a horse will form a single creature with it and will inspire it with his wishes. The animal, thus united with the beneficiary, will have a strength and a vigour three times those that it possesses in its ordinary state.

The beneficiary transformed into a fly, for example, and carried on an eagle's back, will form a single creature with this eagle.

Article 13

The beneficiary will not be able to steal; if he were to try, his organs would refuse to serve him. He will be able to kill ten human beings a year; but nobody to whom he has spoken. For the first year, he can kill a person, so long as he hasn't addressed him on more than two different occasions.

Article 14

If the beneficiary were to wish to relate or were in fact to divulge one of the articles of his privilege, his mouth would be unable to form a single sound, and he would have toothache for twenty-four hours.

Article 15

The beneficiary taking a ring on his finger and saying, 'I pray that harmful insects will be annihilated,' all the insects, six metres away from his ring, in every direction, will be struck dead. These insects are fleas, bugs, lice of all kinds, crab-lice, gnats, flies, rats, etc., etc.

Snakes, vipers, lions, tigers, wolves and all poisonous animals will take flight, overcome by fear, and they will run a league away.

Article 16

In every place, the beneficiary, after saying, 'I pray for my food,' will find: two pounds of bread, a beefsteak medium rare, a leg of mutton ditto, a bottle of St-Julien, a carafe of water, a fruit, an ice-cream and a small cup of coffee. This prayer will be granted twice within twenty-four hours.

Article 17

Ten times a year, on request, the beneficiary will never miss the object he is trying to hit, either with a rifle shot or a pistol shot, or a shot from any other weapon.

Ten times a year, he will fence with twice the strength of the man he is fighting or pitting his strength against; but he will not be able to inflict a wound that leads to death, pain, or discomfort for more than one hundred hours.

Article 18

Ten times a year, the beneficiary, on request, will be able to lessen by three quarters the pain felt by a person he sees; or, if this person is on the point of death, he will be able to prolong his or her life by ten days, lessening their present pain by three quarters. He will be able, on request, to obtain for that suffering person a sudden and painless death.

Article 19

The beneficiary will be able to change a dog into a beautiful or ugly woman; this woman will give him her arm and will have the degree of wit of Mme Ancilla and the heart of Mélanie[4]. This miracle will be renewable twenty times each year.

The beneficiary will be able to change a dog into a man, who will always have the appearance of Pépin de Bellisle, and the wit of *** (the Jewish doctor).

Article 20

The beneficiary will never be more unhappy than he was from the 1st of August 1839 to the 1st of April 1840.[5]

Two hundred times a year, the beneficiary will be able to reduce his sleep to two hours that will produce the same physical effects as eight hours. He will have the eyes of a lynx and the agility of Deburau[6].

Article 21

Twenty times a year, the beneficiary will be able to divine the thoughts of all the people around him, to a distance of twenty paces. – A hundred and twenty times a year, he will be able to see what the person he has chosen is doing at that moment; the woman he loves the most is completely excluded. Dirty and disgusting actions are also excluded.

Article 22

The beneficiary will not be able to earn any money, other than his sixty francs a day, by means of the privileges mentioned above. A hundred and fifty times a year, he will be able to obtain, on request, that a particular person completely forgets him, the beneficiary.

Article 23

Ten times a year, the beneficiary will be transported wherever he likes, at a speed of one hour for every hundred leagues; during the journey he will sleep.

NOTES

These 'privileges' were written on 10th April 1840, two years before Stendhal's death.

1. Written in English.
2. *Mentula*: penis (Latin).
3. General de Belle was famous for his handsomeness. (His name may have reminded Stendhal ironically of his own 'real' name, Beyle.)
4. Mme Ancilla: Stendhal's name for Virginie Ancelot (1792–1875), a writer. Mélanie (Guilbert) was a woman loved by Stendhal in 1804–5.
5. Probably a reference to Stendhal's time with his mistress Giulia Rinieri.
6. Jean Gaspard Deburau (1796–1846), the famous mime.

Stendhal was born Marie-Henri Beyle in Grenoble in 1783. He had an unhappy childhood, disliking both his father and the strict Jesuit atmosphere of their household, and so moved to Paris at his first opportunity. There his relatives found him a position at the Ministry of War and in 1800 he entered Napoleon's army. He served in both Italy and in the failed Russian campaign of 1812. After Napoleon's fall in 1814, Stendhal moved to Milan and it was here that he embarked upon his literary career.

He began publishing under the name Stendhal in 1817 with his travel book, *Rome, Naples and Florence in 1817*. This was better received in England than in his native France, and so he wrote a number of articles for British journals. By 1821 he was back in Paris and heavily involved with Countess Clémentine Curial who sent him some 215 letters during their two-year affair. This relationship led to his work *De l'amour* [*On Love*] (1822), a psychological analysis of love. This was followed by *Armance* (1827), his first novel, and one very coolly received by critics.

His most famous work, *Le Rouge et le Noir* [*The Red and the Black*], appeared in 1831. A complex novel, this explored the French society of the early nineteenth century, with the 'red' symbolising the army, and the 'black' the church. His second masterpiece *La Chartreuse de Parme* [*The Charterhouse of Parma*] was published in 1839, and was immediately praised by Balzac. From 1841 Stendhal went on sick-leave from his post, but he was in fact never to recover, and he died in March 1842, having suffered a fit in the street.

Andrew Brown studied at the University of Cambridge, where he taught French for many years. He now works as a freelance teacher and translator. He is the author of *Roland Barthes: the Figures of Writing* (OUP, 1993) and his translations include Zola's *For a Night of Love*, Gautier's *The Jinx*, Hoffmann's *Mademoiselle de Scudéri*, and Gide's *Theseus*, all published by Hesperus Press.

HESPERUS PRESS – 100 PAGES

Hesperus Press, as suggested by the Latin motto, is committed to bringing near what is far – far both in space and time. Works written by the greatest authors, and unjustly neglected or simply little known in the English-speaking world, are made accessible through new translations and a completely fresh editorial approach. Through these short classic works, each around 100 pages in length, the reader will be introduced to the greatest writers from all times and all cultures.

For more information on Hesperus Press, please visit our website:
www.hesperuspress.com

ET REMOTISSIMA PROPE

SELECTED TITLES FROM HESPERUS PRESS

Gustave Flaubert *Memoirs of a Madman*

Alexander Pope *Scriblerus*

Ugo Foscolo *Last Letters of Jacopo Ortis*

Anton Chekhov *The Story of a Nobody*

Joseph von Eichendorff *Life of a Good-for-nothing*

Mark Twain *The Diary of Adam and Eve*

Giovanni Boccaccio *Life of Dante*

Victor Hugo *The Last Day of a Condemned Man*

Joseph Conrad *Heart of Darkness*

Edgar Allan Poe *Eureka*

Emile Zola *For a Night of Love*

Daniel Defoe *The King of Pirates*

Giacomo Leopardi *Thoughts*

Nikolai Gogol *The Squabble*

Franz Kafka *Metamorphosis*

Herman Melville *The Enchanted Isles*

Leonardo da Vinci *Prophecies*

Charles Baudelaire *On Wine and Hashish*

William Makepeace Thackeray *Rebecca and Rowena*

Wilkie Collins *Who Killed Zebedee?*

Théophile Gautier *The Jinx*

Charles Dickens *The Haunted House*

Luigi Pirandello *Loveless Love*

Fyodor Dostoevsky *Poor People*

E.T.A. Hoffmann *Mademoiselle de Scudéri*

Henry James *In the Cage*

Francis Petrarch *My Secret Book*

André Gide *Theseus*

D.H. Lawrence *The Fox*

Percy Bysshe Shelley *Zastrozzi*

Marquis de Sade *Incest*

Oscar Wilde *The Portrait of Mr W.H.*

Giacomo Casanova *The Duel*

Leo Tolstoy *Hadji Murat*